Tuition

A SUPPLEMENTAL STATEMENT TO THE REPORT
OF THE CARNEGIE COMMISSION ON HIGHER EDUCATION
ON 'WHO PAYS? WHO BENEFITS? WHO SHOULD PAY?'

Prepared by the staff of
The Carnegie Commission on Higher Education

This report is issued by the Carnegie Commission on Higher Education, with headquarters at 2150 Shattuck Avenue, Berkeley, California 94704. The views and conclusions expressed in this statement are solely those of the members of the staff of the Carnegie Commission on Higher Education and do not necessarily reflect the views or opinions of the Carnegie Corporation of New York, The Carnegie Foundation for the Advancement of Teaching, or their trustees, officers, directors, or employees.

TUITION

Printed in the United States of America.

Library of Congress catalog card number 74-78943

Contents

1. Policy Issues to be Resolved

In its earliest report, *Quality and Equality,* the Carnegie Commission on Higher Education had urged that the federal government increase its support of students, particularly students from low-income families. In a later report, *The Capitol and the Campus,* the Commission made recommendations for the levels of state support, both in general and for the private sector. But the Commission had not examined in their totality the broad problems of costs and benefits in higher education. Since these problems are central to objectives of social justice and social effectiveness, the Commission undertook to examine them.

This examination was based on extensive data. Their implications were studied in several meetings. In July 1973, the Commission issued a 190-page report entitled *Higher Education: Who Pays? Who Benefits? Who Should Pay?* It covered a wide range of complicated issues and included substantial statistical analysis in some 52 tables.

The most obvious conclusion derived from the deliberations was that the questions: Who pays? Who benefits? Who should pay? involve a number of important and interrelated issues. Therefore, the Commission did not make a single recommendation, but instead concluded that to achieve the objectives of social justice and social effectiveness, and to channel public subsidies most effectively, eight policy directions should be followed. The eight directions for financing of higher education endorsed by the Commission were:

A short-term increase in the public share of monetary costs for higher education to be followed by a long-term increase in the private share until it again reaches about current proportions

A redistribution of the governmental burden from the states and localities toward the federal government

A redistribution of student subsidies from higher- to lower-income groups

A greater amount of support for private colleges and universities

A comparative, although modest and gradual, rise in public as against private tuition

A reevaluation of tuition policy to gear it more to the actual costs of education by level of the training

Greater reliance on better loan programs in the longer-run future and on charges to users

Careful conservation in the use of resources to minimize the rising impact on the GNP

And the report noted: "We also are concerned that the totality of funds available to higher education be adequate."

In order to emphasize the interrelatedness of the eight policy directions, the Commission added: "These recommendations should be considered all at once, and no one recommendation should be taken out of context of this total additive approach to financing—for example, the raising of tuition without an increase in student aid."

In the months since the report was issued, nothing has happened to change the importance of these eight policy directions. But the Commission's urging that the recommendations be considered as a whole has not been very influential. Indeed, only two of the eight suggested directions have given rise to substantial public controversy and they have often been discussed as isolated recommendations withdrawn from the total "package":

1 "A redistribution of student subsidies from higher- to lower-income groups." Students now receive subsidies from two sources: (a) tuition at rates below educational costs, and (b) student aid through grants, subsidized loans and work-study. Tuition subsidies, by themselves, particularly advantage higher- and middle-income groups since, without student aid, young persons from lower-income groups often cannot afford to attend college even with low or even no tuition. Student aid targeted to need, on the other hand, particularly advantages lower- and middle-income groups. The Commission, at all times, favored greater access to college by young persons from lower- and middle-income groups. Thus it supported somewhat less emphasis on across-the-board tuition subsidies and more attention to student aid targeted to lower- and middle-income families. In total, the Commission favored *more* student subsidies, along with a redistribution of them by income level by means of increasing the proportion distributed by way of targeted student aid (see Chart 1).

The Commission stated: "We favor a gradual redistribution of subsidies (a) by charging higher tuition to those who can afford to pay it—rising gradually over a period of years; and (b) by providing more aid to students from lower-income families, particularly through the full funding of the Basic Opportunity Grants program provided by the Education Amendments of 1972, and through liberalization, for lower-division students, of the limitation on the proportion of student costs that can be covered."[1]

2 "A . . . modest and gradual rise in public as against private tuition." Public tuition is now estimated to be about 24 percent of educational costs; and private tuition to be about 62 percent of educational costs. This current gap is considerably wider than general historical practice in absolute money terms, as the general level of tuition has risen.

CHART 1 Student subsidies from public sources, estimated 1973-74

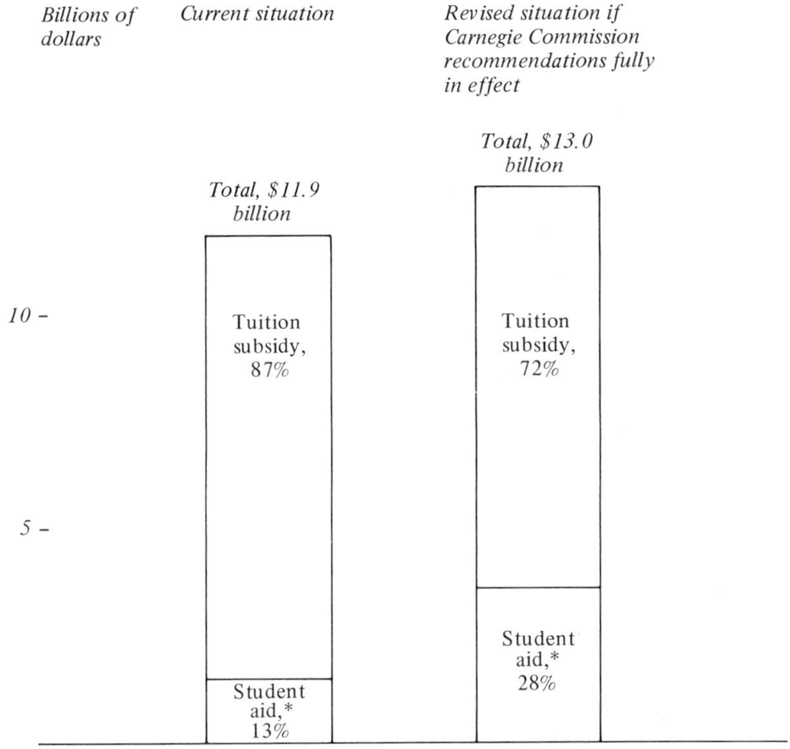

Billions of dollars

Current situation

Revised situation if Carnegie Commission recommendations fully in effect

Total, $13.0 billion

Total, $11.9 billion

10 –

Tuition subsidy, 87%

Tuition subsidy, 72%

5 –

Student aid,* 28%

Student aid,* 13%

*Excludes veterans' benefits, social security benefits, and cost of loans.

SOURCES: Adapted from U.S. Office of Education data by Carnegie Commission staff; for estimate of cost of student aid under Carnegie Commission recommendations and reasons for omissions, see Table 1.

[1]This 1972 program currently provides aid for students from families with incomes up to about $12,000 under normal circumstances, and up to about $18,000 under exceptional circumstances. The program has been inadequately funded to date and the level of family income covered has been set too low.

As a consequence of these two policy considerations, but particularly of the first one, the Commission specifically suggested that, where it had not yet done so, tuition in public four-year institutions might rise, over a ten-year period, to a level of about one-third of "educational costs."[2] The Commission exempted two-year colleges from any suggested increases, favoring low, or preferably no tuition for them. These two-year colleges represent about 30 percent of all enrollments. The Commission also recommended very substantial increases, at both the state and federal levels, in student aid subsidies (see Table 1).[3]

The report of the Commission came out at about the same time as other reports on the same range of issues, and, understandably, there has been some confusion among them. The several reports taken together, however, do reflect the rising concern with the amount and the form of student subsidies at both the state and federal levels. Many states have raised tuition substantially in recent years, as have private institutions. Student aid has been undergoing even greater changes at both the state and, especially, the federal level.

The current debate, particularly about changing practices but also about the several reports making policy recommendations, was probably inevitable and it should have constructive consequences. In the course of this debate, the issues, the facts, and the alternatives are being clarified.

This debate takes place as the historical system of student subsidy from public funds (low or no tuition across-the-board for students at public institutions made possible by state budgetary support, and no direct public subsidy for students at private institutions) is now being increasingly challenged by a developing system of student subsidy (more of the subsidy through financial aid directly to students on the basis of need at both public and private institutions). Several central issues arise:

(1) Should support of higher education be more through students or more through institutions?

(2) Should support be available for attendance at private as well as at public institutions?

[2]Educational costs are defined to include those expenditures classified by the U.S. Office of Education as "educational and general" expenses. Included are instruction and departmental research; extension and public service; libraries; general administration, general institutional expense, and student services; organized activities relating to educational departments; other sponsored programs; and all other educational and general expense. Excluded are auxiliary enterprises, student aid, and capital improvements, as well as all organized research. Auxiliary enterprises are comprised of such activities as the operation of residence halls and dining rooms.

[3]All tables are shown in the Statistical Appendix.

(3) Should support be directed more toward students drawn from lower- and middle-income families or should it be provided equally for students from all families regardless of income and including many who otherwise can afford to attend?

(4) What should be the total financial burden of each approach and what should be its distribution among federal and state and local governments on the one hand, and families and students on the other?

Because the Commission's recommendations on tuition, in particular, have been isolated from the rest of the issues in the present debate and have become the subject of public controversy, the Commission staff[4] has decided to issue this supplemental statement.

The statement neither changes nor modifies the recommendations of the Commission on tuition or on any other issue. It seeks, rather, to do the following:

1 Restate the reasons for the Commission's recommendations on tuition

2 Provide more recent and more precise information

3 Indicate more clearly the potential impacts of its suggestion for modestly higher average tuition at public four-year institutions by presenting data by type of institution and by state

4 Contrast and compare the Commission's recommendations with those of the Committee for Economic Development, and of other selected bodies

5 Comment on certain current controversies about tuition policy

6 Note some of the many complexities of getting equity in tuition policy

[4]Acknowledgment is made particularly of the assistance of Margaret S. Gordon and Steve Murphy.

2. Reasons for the Commission's Recommendations on Tuition

Why did the Commission recommend a change in historic tuition policy in public four-year institutions?

The basic reason is that public subsidies can be channeled to students who need assistance more effectively through a combination of modest tuition charges and student aid than through primary reliance on very low or no tuition.[1] When students are subsidized primarily through very low or no tuition, the benefits flow to all students attending public four-year institutions regardless of family income. In other words, the benefits flow to many students who could well afford to pay at least a modest tuition charge, whereas through a combination of modest tuition charges and student aid a more significant portion of public subsidy funds would specifically aid those students who, in terms of family income, are most in need of assistance (see Chart 2).

An additional consideration is that in many states, middle- and upper-income families benefit, not only from low tuition at public institutions, but also from regressive state tax structures that impose a disproportionately heavy tax burden on low-income families.

A low tuition policy by itself tends to channel more subsidies to higher-income groups in total because more young persons attend college from those groups. A targeted student aid policy by itself tends to channel more subsidies to lower-income groups in total because they are the ones to whom the aid is targeted and more of them attend when aid is available. Current policy, which combines some elements of each

[1]This is under current conditions where students from all family income ranges attend public institutions. In earlier times, when students from wealthier families tended to go to private institutions with higher tuition and students from less affluent families tended to go to public institutions with lower tuition, then tuition charges, in fact, more nearly reflected ability to pay and subsidies more nearly reflected need. In recent times, however, the public sector has not only grown greatly in proportion to the private but its quality has greatly improved. Not so long ago only a few public universities (such as Michigan, Texas, and California) attracted students from throughout the income range; now many public institutions and colleges do so. No longer is low or no tuition at public institutions only for the "deserving poor." Both public and private institutions are now less identified by the income levels of the students in attendance.

CHART 2 Two illustrative policies* for student subsidies: impact by family income group

Subsidy	*Policy A* *No tuition across-the-board*	*Policy B* *Modest tuition and student assistance combined (tuition=$700)*		Subsidy
		Tuition subsidy	Student aid	
Upper-income student	$2,100			$1,400
Upper-middle-income student	2,100			1,400
Middle-middle-income student	2,100		900	2,300
Lower-middle-income student	2,100		1,200	2,600
Lower-income student	2,100		1,400	2,800
Total cost	$10,500	7,000	3,500	$10,500

*The illustrations are particularly relevant for a state university, where the cost of education for a student is likely to be about $2,100; tuition subsidies would tend to be somewhat lower in other four-year institutions and in two-year institutions. We refer here to the estimated cost per full-time equivalent undergraduate. The total cost is for five students—one from each income quintile.

NOTE: This chart is purely illustrative. Policy B goes beyond current eligibility provisions of the Basic Opportunity Grants program.

approach, channels somewhat more total aid proportionately to higher-income groups. The recommendations of the Carnegie Commission would more nearly balance subsidies among income levels (see Chart 3). In economic terms, the low tuition policy by itself is moderately "regressive"; the targeted aid policy is highly "progressive"; the current mixture is modestly "regressive"; and the Carnegie Commission approach is more nearly modestly "progressive"—each in terms of dis-

CHART 3 Distribution of public subsidy funds benefiting undergraduates, by family income quintile, under four alternative assumptions

Family income quintile	A. *Existing public tuition subsidies only**	B. *Basic Opportunity Grants program only +*
V (highest)	27%	
IV	23%	
III	16%	10%
II	16%	30%
I (lowest)	18%	60%

Family income quintile	C. *Existing public tuition subsidies and student aid‡*	D. *Public tuition subsidies and student aid under full implementation of Carnegie Commission recommendations §*
V	24%	19%
IV	22%	18%
III	17%	17%
II	18%	21%
I	19%	25%

*Includes tuition subsidies at public institutions and estimated tuition subsidies from public funds at private institutions.

+Assumes total annual expenditures of $1.3 billion, as recommended by the federal administration for 1974-75, and existing eligibility standards.

‡Includes total estimated tuition subsidies and student aid from public funds at public and private institutions.

§ Includes modified tuition subsidies at public institutions, estimated tuition subsidies from public funds at private institutions, and total student aid from public funds, including increases recommended by the Commission.

SOURCES: Estimated by Carnegie Commission staff from U.S. Office of Education, U.S. Bureau of the Census, and California State Scholarship and Loan Commission data.

tribution of subsidies. (For the distribution of *total* subsidies, not public alone, see Chart A in the Statistical Appendix.)

Why did the Commission recommend limiting tuition increases in public four-year institutions so that, by 1983, tuition revenue would equal about one-third of educational costs?

Essentially, there were three reasons:

1. The situation that has evolved historically, in which students and their families meet approximately one-third of total institutional educational costs,[2] is generally equitable, as was explained in the earlier report.
2. More pronounced increases in tuition in public four-year institutions than were recommended would place undue burdens on students from middle-income and upper-middle-income families.
3. The suggested level of tuition as a percentage of educational costs at public four-year institutions seemed to be reasonably related to current two-year levels (about 17 percent) and current private four-year levels (about 62 percent).

Some of those who have commented on the Carnegie Commission's recommendations on tuition policy have implied that the major purpose of the Commission was to facilitate the survival of private colleges and universities by reducing the gap between their tuition charges and those of competing public institutions. Lowering this gap was not the major purpose of the recommendation, although it would be a result of its implementation. The Commission did not regard reducing the tuition gap as the main pathway to survival of private institutions. In several reports, especially *The Capitol and the Campus* and *Higher Education: Who Pays? Who Benefits? Who Should Pay?*, the Commission strongly recommended state aid to private institutions of higher education, chiefly through grants to students based on need, to offset, in part or in whole, higher tuition charges. A quotation from the latter report:

> We believe that the states should increasingly support private institutions in ways that best preserve institutional independence, and that

[2]Total institutional educational costs include those costs that flow through the accounts of institutions of higher education. They do not include students' foregone earnings, that is, the earnings students might receive if they were not spending their time in classrooms and libraries. It is estimated that students and their parents meet approximately two-thirds of total economic costs of higher education, including foregone earnings (Carnegie Commission 1973b, p. 2). This private payment of two-thirds of economic costs was considered generally balanced by private benefits received; as against public payment of one-third of economic costs balanced against public benefits received. Payment of one-third of institutional educational costs results in payment of two-thirds of economic costs.

also make possible, in particular, the attendance of more students from low-income families. We especially favor aid through students in order to help preserve the independence of the private institutions and to increase the options open to students. . . . Federal funding of the State Incentive Grants program in the Higher Education Act of 1972 would encourage the states to embark upon or expand such programs.

3. More Recent and More Precise Information

Revenue from tuition and other required fees amounted to at least 23 percent of educational costs for undergraduate students at public four-year institutions in 1971-72 (Table 2). It is estimated that the corresponding percentage is at least 24 percent in 1973-74. In fact, as we shall see later, after further adjusting for the high costs of advanced graduate education and medical education, the estimated percentage of 1971-72 is about 26 to 27 percent in terms of undergraduate students; and thus 27 or 28 percent in 1973-74. The earlier report of the Commission used a figure of 17 percent for all students in 1973.[1]

[1]The reasons for the difference between the 17 percent figure earlier used and the 24 percent figure are as follows:

(1) More recent financial data. The 17 percent figure utilized data for 1969-70; the 24 percent figure utilizes data two years more current—1971-72.

(2) More recent tuition data. The 17 percent figure assumed that public tuition would keep on rising between 1969-70 and 1973 at its customary rate. It has risen faster.

(3) Corrected data. The Carnegie Commission staff found major errors in the basic sources affecting two large systems—New York State and Massachusetts State.

(4) Adjustments to reflect the situation for undergraduates at four-year institutions. This is what the Commission was basically concerned with, as has been the public discussion. The Commission eliminated the community colleges from its one-third suggested policy. It was largely silent about the very complex issues of tuition at advanced graduate levels which vary greatly among fields. Thus: (a) the two-year colleges are not now included and (b) organized research is also not now included (one quarter was included previously) on the grounds that it relates to the education of advanced graduate students.

(5) Use of actual expenditures instead of income. This is a minor factor. Expenditures have exceeded income in some situations.

The seven percentage points between 17 and 24 are explained almost equally by (a) more recent and corrected data, (b) the exclusion of community colleges, and (c) the exclusion of one-quarter of organized research.

The 27 or 28 percent figure exceeds the 24 percent figure by three or four percentage points because of additional adjustments designed to eliminate the effect of the high cost of advanced graduate and medical education. These last adjustments are based on the most general of estimates and thus are more uncertain in their amounts. (See Technical Note in the Statistical Appendix.)

A rise from the low figure of 24 percent to 33 percent over ten years is considerably less than a rise from 17 percent. To reach the recommended one-third level by 1983 would mean that tuition revenue would have to rise, on the average, by about 1 percent of educational costs per year, over and above the amount required to maintain the current ratio of tuition revenue to educational costs (or an average additional rise of less than $20 per year per student in current dollars). Application of the higher percentages, of course, leads to smaller prospective increases.

In any event, in calculating the possible impact of the recommendations of the Carnegie Commission over the next ten years, it should be accepted that tuition for undergraduates at four-year institutions now averages at least 24 percent and possibly as much as 28 percent.

Historically, tuition (in constant dollars) has tended to rise at about the same rate as real per capita disposable personal income in the long run, though not necessarily in the short run (Chart 4 and Table 3). Thus, the Commission's recommendation would result in an average rise of tuition in public four-year institutions that would exceed the rise in per capita disposable income slightly until 1983 and then resume the historical relationship to increases in per capita income. In other words, the increase recommended is both "modest and gradual." The rise in per capita disposable income is a good rough measure both of rising ability to pay and of rising educational costs on campus.

CHART 4 **Average annual rise in tuition at public and private colleges and universities, and in per capita income, 1929-30 to 1973-74 (in constant dollars)**

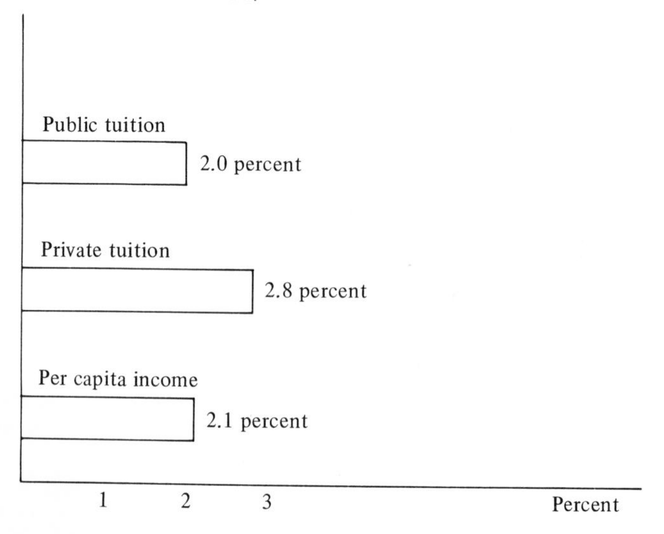

SOURCE: Table 3

Another point brought out dramatically in Table 3 is that tuition in private institutions has been rising considerably more rapidly than per capita income since the late 1950s (except in the last few years), and this helps to explain the growing tuition gap between private and public institutions. This comparatively rapid rise in private tuition was the main reason why the Commission said that private tuition in the future should rise "at a somewhat slower rate" than per capita disposable income; and, in this fashion, the private institutions could make their own contributions to reducing what has been a widening gap. Thus the Commission, in total, made three suggestions for narrowing the public-private gap: first, and most important, state support should be made available to private institutions; second, the rate of rise of private tuition that marked the 1960s should be slowed down; and third, there should be a "modest and gradual" rise of public tuition on the average.

Overall, the new data show a much closer correspondence between current practice and the Commission recommendation for 1983 than did the earlier report.

4. *Disaggregation of Data by Type of Institution*

Nationwide, the percentage of educational costs covered by tuition is remarkably similar among categories of public institutions with the exception of "liberal arts colleges"—very few in number—and two-year institutions—exempted from any increases in the Commission's recommendation (see Chart 5).

The ratios of private to public percentages of educational costs covered by tuition, within each category, however, vary considerably. This is because tuition covers a much larger percentage of educational costs at some types of private institutions than it does at others—81 percent at "comprehensive colleges and universities" but only 36 percent at "research universities I" (see Table 2).[1]

[1] For a description of the classification of institutions of higher education on which the types of institutions included in Table 2 are based, see Carnegie Commission (1973a). The institutions included are those listed in the U.S. Office of Education's report on opening fall enrollment for 1970 (U.S. National Center for Educational Statistics, 1971).

CHART 5 **Revenue from tuition and required fees as a percentage of educational costs, by type and control of institution, 1971-72**

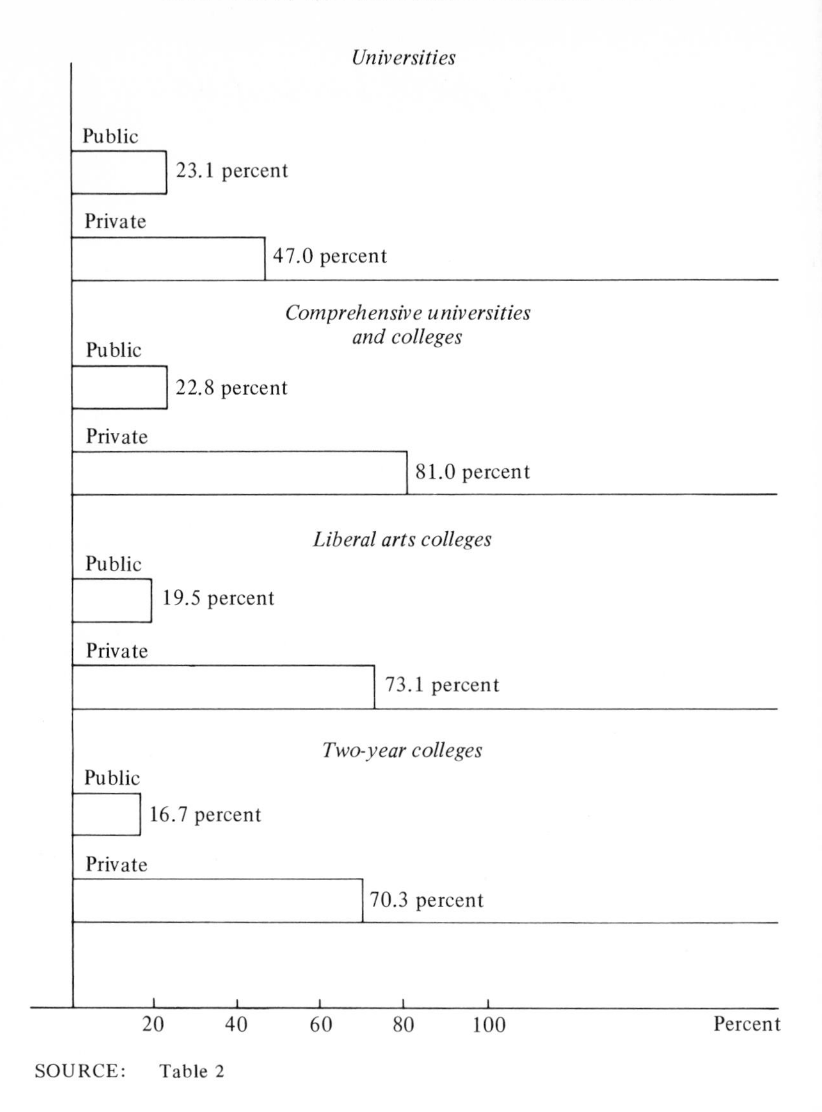

SOURCE: Table 2

5. *Disaggregation of Data by State*

The situation varies substantially from state to state (see Chart 6). Pennsylvania has a much higher level of tuition revenue relative to educational costs, for example, than does Texas (see Table 4).

Great variations also exist within states. In some states (as in California) revenue from tuition and fees at two-year institutions covers a much lower percentage of educational costs than at other institutions;[1] but in other states (as in Georgia) it covers a higher percentage. Tuition revenue covers a higher percentage of educational costs at "universities" than at "comprehensive colleges and universities" in some states (as in California) but a lower percentage in others (again as in Georgia, among others). In at least one state (New York) there are two quite distinctive comprehensive public systems, one with a policy of no tuition but some required fees (the City University of New York) and the other with tuition (the State University of New York). Thus, at four-year CUNY colleges revenue from required fees averaged about 15 percent of educational expenditures; while at SUNY, revenues from tuition and required fees covered about 18 percent at university campuses, and about 27 percent at four-year colleges in 1971-72.

National figures fail to disclose the enormous variations of policies and practices among and within the states. Some states (such as Pennsylvania) are already at or above the general level of public tuition revenue as a percentage of educational costs at public institutions recommended for 1983 by the Carnegie Commission, while others are much farther below this level than the national averages might imply. Also within states, some categories of institutions are much closer to the suggested 1983 level than are others (for example, the "comprehensive colleges and universities" in Georgia are closer to the recommended levels than are the "universities").

Table 5 illustrates quite graphically the many variations among insti-

[1] Actually, California community colleges do not charge tuition but do have some modest fees.

CHART 6 **Distribution of "comprehensive universities and colleges" by average level of tuition and required fees as a percentage of educational costs in each state, 1971-72**

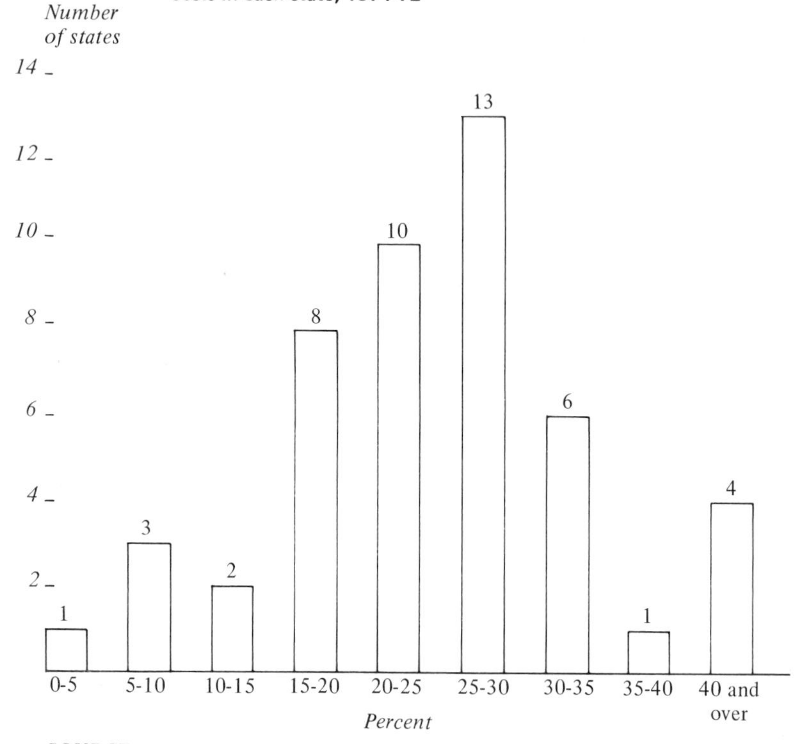

SOURCE: Table 4

tutions by showing the percentage of educational costs covered by tuition and fee receipts at the main campus of each land-grant institution—or, in some cases, the system as a whole (see Chart 7). For some of these institutions, given the recent rate of actual rise in tuition, the recommendation of the Commission for 1983 would quite obviously serve more as a ceiling guideline than as a floor, and is already a proposed "lid" for some which are above the suggested 1983 level.

Actually, variations in ratios of tuition revenue to educational costs from state to state do not altogether accurately reflect differences in tuition policy, especially among universities. Some state universities attract relatively more students from out of the state than do others, a factor which tends to increase tuition revenue because of the higher tuition charges for nonresidents. On the other hand, universities with relatively high proportions of advanced graduate students are likely to

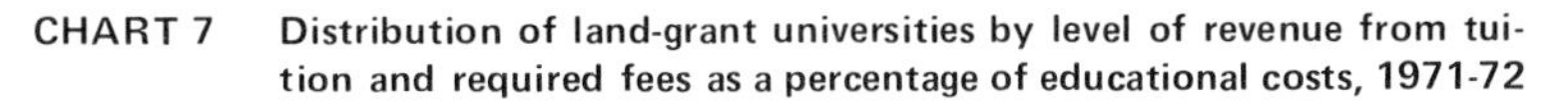

CHART 7 Distribution of land-grant universities by level of revenue from tuition and required fees as a percentage of educational costs, 1971-72

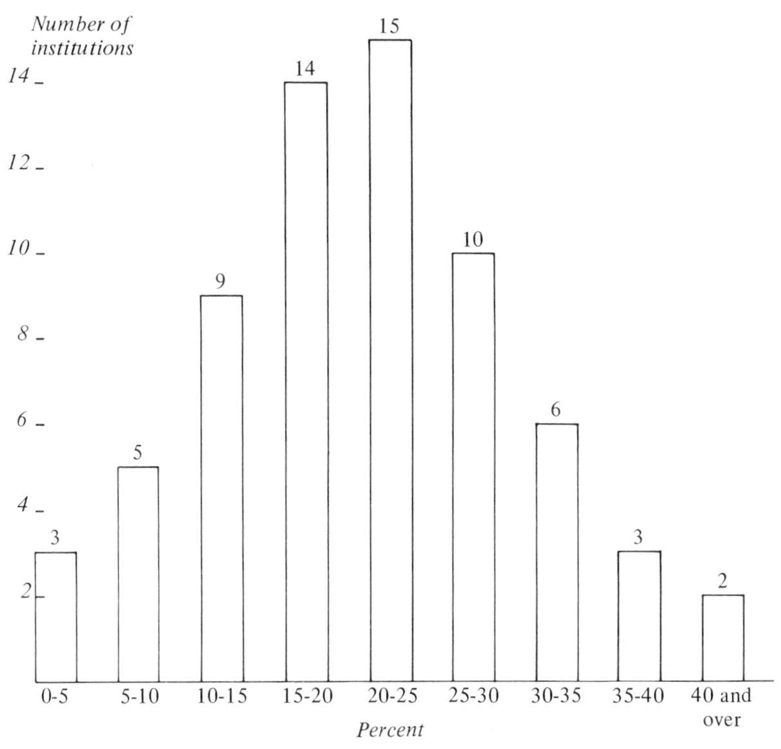

SOURCE: Table 5

have correspondingly high costs, a factor that depresses the ratio of tuition revenue to educational costs.

The University of Michigan, where tuition and fee revenue represented 29.9 percent of educational costs in 1971-72, is a good example of an institution affected by both of these factors, which tend to work in opposite directions. However, largely as a result of court decisions which led the university to permit nonresident students to pay resident tuition after a waiting period of one year as a student, tuition for both residents and nonresidents was raised sharply in the fall of 1973 in an attempt to offset the anticipated decline in tuition revenue from nonresident students. The increase for resident lower-division students was 15 percent and for resident upper-division students, 30 percent. Total revenue from tuition and fees was expected to amount to 31.8 percent of educational costs in 1973-74—not much more than in 1971-72 because tuition revenue from resident and nonresident students combined would not be greatly increased by the rise in tuition charges.[2]

These complications, which are discussed more fully in the Statistical Appendix, do not affect interstate comparisons among public "comprehensive universities and colleges" or among "liberal arts colleges" as seriously because their students are likely to be state residents, for the most part, while their graduate students are relatively less numerous and tend to be at the master's level, where educational costs are considerably lower than for doctoral candidates.

At the universities, however, several factors, in addition to those already mentioned, distort comparisons: (1) tuition tends to be the same for graduate students as for undergraduates, although costs are substantially higher; (2) tuition is often not charged to research assistants and to graduate students who are teaching assistants; (3) medical school costs, when included, greatly increase total educational costs while medical schools add little to tuition revenue. Thus, the overall percentage for a university may not be at all indicative of percentages for undergraduates and for M.A. candidates, if these could be disentangled. As an example, tuition and fees for undergraduates at the University of California are four times as high as they are at the California State University and Colleges, but the percentage of educational costs covered by tuition revenues is less than twice as high for the reasons given above (20.1 percent versus 13.5 percent. See Table 4).[3] Generally, the percentages for universities are lower or even substantially lower than if only undergraduate tuition-fee revenue and undergraduate educational costs were included in the data. Comparisons among universities and between universities and other types of institutions, thus, must be made only with the greatest of care to understand the specific circumstances.

Because of these complications, we have attempted to estimate the percentage of undergraduate educational costs covered by tuition and required fees, using several alternative methods of eliminating the effect of the high costs associated with graduate education (especially at the

[2]Earlier the University of Michigan had permitted nonresidents to qualify for in-state tuition charges only after living six months in the state while not a student (Van Dyne, 1973, p. 5). Not only the University of Michigan, but many other state institutions as well, are being affected by liberalization of the rules for acquiring residency status that have been associated with the lowering of the legal age of adulthood and related court decisions. We are indebted to budget analysts at the University of Michigan for 1973-74 data on tuition revenue and expenditures.

[3]The University of California campuses with medical schools tend to have low percentages—Davis, 15.8 percent; Irvine, 21.7 percent; Los Angeles, 19.2 percent; and San Diego, 10.0 percent. Those without medical schools generally have higher percentages—Berkeley, 27.2 percent; Riverside, 18.9 percent; Santa Barbara, 28.7 percent; and Santa Cruz, 27.3 percent.

doctoral candidate stage) and of the even higher costs of medical education. The results suggest that, on the average, in universities and other four-year public institutions, about 26 to 27 percent of undergraduate costs were covered by tuition and required fees in 1971-72, as compared with the 23 percent shown in Table 2 without these adjustments. (The percentage in universities alone may be about 30 percent. See Technical Note in Statistical Appendix.)

To provide an indication of how actual undergraduate tuition charges vary among state systems, data have been assembled for the years from 1971-72 to 1973-74 in Tables 6 and 7. Table 6, which relates to tuition for state residents, suggests the following:

(1) There is a rough tendency for actual tuition charges to vary among state systems in much the same manner as the percentages shown in Table 4, but there are some exceptions.

(2) In many states, tuition at "comprehensive universities and colleges" is only slightly below that at universities (or at the one state university), and in a few cases it is actually higher.

(3) In some states, tuition charges vary little or not at all among "comprehensive universities and colleges," whereas in others there is surprisingly wide variation. In this connection, however, it is important to note that in a number of states tuition at public black colleges—colleges founded for Negroes—is exceptionally low, and this is one factor in explaining variations within state systems.

(4) There is some tendency toward regional variations in tuition charges. For example, they tend to be low to moderate in the Southern states, whereas they tend to be high in the Northeast (extending into such Northeast Central states as Michigan and Ohio). In the Northeast region, however, there are exceptions—tuition charges tend to be moderate in Massachusetts and Maine, while the City University of New York has only modest fees, but no tuition, for residents of New York City. The lower tuition charges in the South are partly explained by lower costs.

(5) The practice of charging lower tuition to lower-division than to upper-division students—recommended by the Carnegie Commission—has modestly begun, and by 1973-74 prevailed at state universities in at least three states (the University of Michigan, the State University of New York, and the University of Wisconsin).

(6) Although there have been many comments about sharp tuition increases in public four-year universities and colleges in the last few years, the data show that these sharp increases have occurred in a

relatively modest proportion of the states, whereas in many others increases have been slight or nonexistent, and there have been a few decreases.

Public institutions of higher education almost universally charge higher tuition to nonresidents than to residents.

(1) Total charges for tuition and fees for nonresidents generally range from two to three times those for residents, but there are some states in which the ratio of nonresident to resident charges is well above three and a few in which it is less than two.

(2) A number of the institutions maintaining exceptionally low charges for residents have unusually high ratios of nonresident to resident charges (e.g., California State University and Colleges, Federal City College, CUNY Queens College,[4] and Texas public institutions).

(3) On the other hand, some of the institutions with comparatively high charges for residents have relatively low ratios of nonresident to resident charges (notably SUNY).

(4) Clearly nonresident tuition and fee charges are substantially closer to those of private colleges than are resident charges.

The disaggregated data show the enormous complexity of the tuition issue state by state and institution by institution. There is no "average" situation. Thus the general guideline suggested by the Commission has very different implications for state systems or for individual institutions where tuition revenue already approximates or even exceeds one-third of educational costs than it does for those where it is below or even far below that level.

[4]At Queens College, and other colleges within the CUNY system, a higher tuition charge was formerly made for nonresidents of New York State than for out-of-city residents of New York City, but this distinction has been discontinued.

6. Recommendations Contrasted and Compared

CARNEGIE COMMISSION AND THE CED

In much of the public discussion, the recommendations of the Carnegie Commission on public tuition have been viewed as substantially identical with those of the Committee for Economic Development (*The Management and Financing of Colleges,* October 1973). A careful reading will show major differences:

	Carnegie Commission	*CED*
Coverage	Four-year institutions	Four-year and two-year institutions
Suggested tuition as percentage of educational costs	33 percent	50 percent[1]
Gap between suggested percentage and estimated current percentage	9 percentage points	26 percentage points
Length of time to reach suggested level	10 years	5 years (10 years for two-year colleges)
Rate at which gap would need to be closed for four-year institutions	1 percentage point per year	5 percentage points per year
Ratio of resulting percentages between private and public four-year institutions (assuming private institutions stay at the 62 percent rate)	Roughly 2 to 1	Roughly 5 to 4

Thus the practical impact of implementation of the CED proposal would be to raise public tuition in relation to educational cost five times as fast as the Carnegie Commission proposal would do during the next five years. Also, the CED proposal would narrow the gap between private and public tuition percentages much below any actual ratio in recent history.

[1] Whether CED was using the same definition of educational costs as was the Carnegie Commission is not entirely clear. Their report (pp. 25 and 69) recommends raising tuitions and fees "until they approximate 50 percent of instructional costs (defined to include a reasonable allowance for replacement of facilities)." In any event, the Carnegie Commission did not include "replacement of facilities."

CEEB The College Entrance Examination Board (*Report of the Committee on Student Economics,* 1972) gives no specific figures but it also stated (1) that parents and students "who can afford to . . . must expect to pay more," and (2) that "the effective difference between the charges of publicly and non-publicly supported institutions" should be "reduced."

NEW YORK STATE The Task Force on Financing Higher Education recommended to Governor Rockefeller (*Higher Education in New York State,* 1973) that (1) tuition charges at public institutions should be uniform throughout the state, (2) low tuition charges (representing about 40 percent of educational costs) should be maintained for the first two years of study, and (3) higher tuition charges (perhaps 50 percent of educational costs) should be maintained for work during the last two undergraduate years.

BOYER Particularly close to the Carnegie Commission recommendations, not only with respect to tuition policy, but also on federal and state support of higher education generally, were the comments of Commissioner Ernest L. Boyer (Chancellor of the State University of New York), submitted as a supplementary statement to the report of the National Commission on the Financing of Postsecondary Education.[2] Commissioner Boyer was joined in these comments by four other members of the National Commission. On tuition policy for public institutions, Boyer's statement recommended (1) that tuition for the first two years should "be free or at least be stabilized at the present level," and (2) that beyond the first two years tuition should be graduated by level and "should remain low in cost (a maximum of approximately one-third of instructional costs might be a useful bench mark) . . . ." Also noteworthy was his recommendation that "private institutions, while receiving their principal support from non-public sources, should be recognized as essential educational resources by each state." He suggested a number of ways in which state governments might appropriately provide financial support to private colleges and universities.

As Roger W. Heyns, President of the American Council on Education, pointed out in commenting on the report of the National Commission, Chancellor Boyer's statement "will be widely endorsed in the higher-education community" (American Council on Education, 1974, p. 4).

PENNSYLVANIA STATE Also consistent with Carnegie Commission recommendations were the proposals recently made by the Pennsylvania Association of Colleges and Universities (1973). (1) Revenue from tuition and fees at public

[2] National Commission on the Financing of Postsecondary Education (1973, pp. 361-367). See Attachment A.

institutions in Pennsylvania is already one-third or slightly more of educational costs, and it is recommended that tuition not be increased. (2) It is proposed that the independent institutions be given $600 a year for each student holding an assistance grant. (3) It is also proposed that the family income ceiling for assistance grants be raised to $20,000.

All of these reports call for very substantially increased assistance to students from low-income families.

7. Current Controversial Questions

Is the middle-class student being forced out by higher tuition?

There is no evidence that this has happened, although no doubt many young people from middle-income families cannot afford to attend the more expensive private colleges and universities today. But the groups that gained ground between 1967 and 1972, as a percentage of all entering freshmen, were young people from the lowest family income quintile (the "lower-income" families), aided especially by increased student aid and affirmative action programs; from the third quintile (the "middle-middle" income families); and from the fourth quintile (the "upper-middle" income families).[1] See Chart 8. It is chiefly young persons from the highest quintile (the "upper" income families) who form a declining proportion (though by no means a declining number) of entering freshmen, but a much higher percentage (34.5) of young persons in this quintile attended college in 1967 than the 20 percent of all families from which they came.

Significantly, between 1972 and 1973, the trends that had largely prevailed since 1967 were reversed. Young persons from the lowest income quintile lost ground as a percentage of entering freshmen, as did those from the next lowest quintile (the "lower-middle" income families). All the other income groups gained ground, and the loss that had previously been experienced in relative representation by the highest quintile was partially reversed.

What is particularly significant about the data in Chart 8 and Table 8 is that the two lowest income groups, and especially the lowest group, form very substantially smaller percentages of freshmen than their families' respective fifths of the population of all families in the United States. Other evidence along the same lines, but compiled in a some-

[1] The lowest quintile consists of those families whose annual dollar income falls in the bottom fifth of income received by all families, the second quintile consists of the next lowest fifth, etc.

CHART 8 Percentage of entering freshmen from each family income quintile, 1967 to 1973

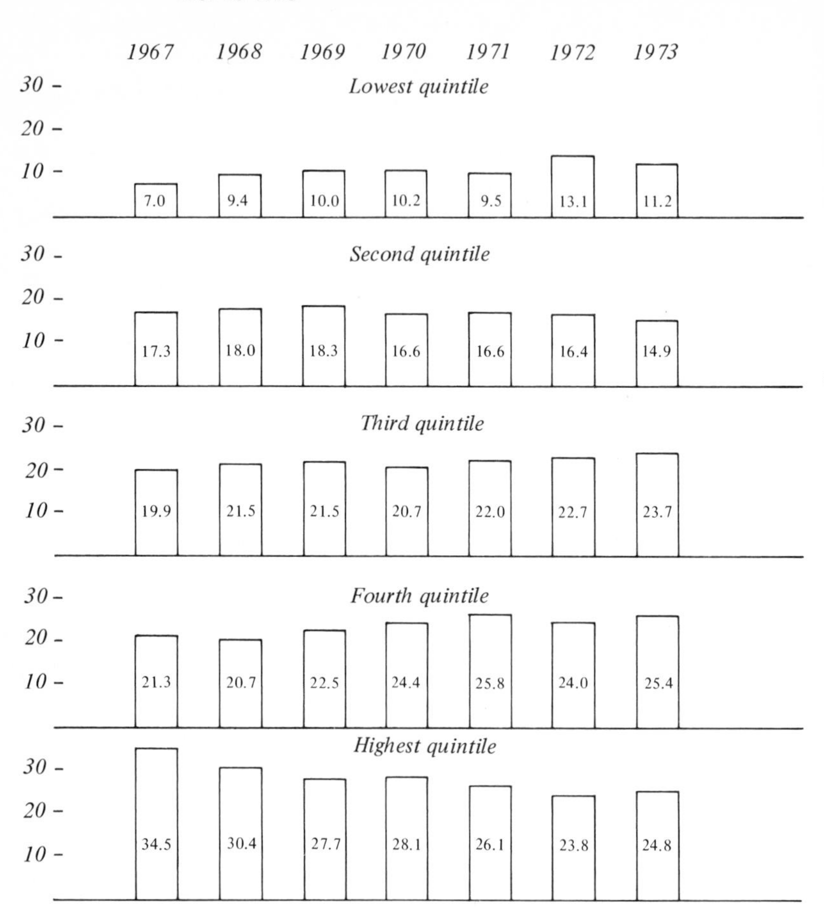

SOURCE: Table 8

what different manner, is provided by Table 9, which compares the family income distributions of all young persons aged 18 to 24 and of collegiate undergraduates in the same age group. Clearly young people from families with incomes below $10,000 form much smaller proportions of college students than of the age group as a whole, whereas the reverse is true for young people from higher income families, and especially for those from families with incomes of $15,000 and up. But even among those from families with incomes of $10,000 to $15,000 (who come close to being the "middle-middle" income families), the proportion of collegiates (29.4 percent) considerably exceeds their representation in the population (25.2 percent).

Nevertheless, young persons from these "middle-middle" income families face difficult financial problems in many cases, and this has been especially true in the last few years when tuition (in current dollars) and subsistence costs have been rising sharply. Only those from the lower portion of this income bracket, i.e. those from families with incomes of $10,000 to $12,000, can under ordinary circumstances qualify for Basic Opportunity Grants, and the amounts they receive are smaller than those received by lower-income students.

College attendance requires some family sacrifice in nearly all situations, and almost certainly for all "middle-middle" income families. Even among "upper-middle" income families, heavy financial sacrifices will be required in some situations, especially if there are several children in college at one time, but this is much less likely to be true for "upper" income families.

The Carnegie Commission at all times has been most concerned that the long-standing and very basic American promise of equality of opportunity be fulfilled in the very near future. Concern for this national commitment, made as early as 1776, animated many of the Commission's reports, and, in the report to which this statement is a supplement, was a major factor in the proposal for comparatively greater support for those elements of the population with relative deprivation in college attendance—the lower-income groups. It is true that a comparative improvement in their educational opportunities requires increased subsidies from other segments of the population and that more graduates coming from families with lower incomes implies more competition in the job market for graduates from families with higher incomes, but disappointment of long-deferred prospects for such comparative improvement also has costs that merit attention.

The *New York Times* in its article, "Minorities Drop in U.S. Colleges: First Slash Since Mid-60's Is Linked to Economics," (February 3, 1974) reported:

> The survey by the American Council on Education showed that 7.8 percent of the 1.6 million freshmen who entered colleges and universities throughout the United States last fall were black. A similar survey of the freshmen who entered in 1972 found that 8.7 percent were black. Until 1973, there had been a steady increase in the black percentage.
>
> In addition, the total portion of all minority group members—Spanish-surnamed, Oriental and American Indian, as well as black—dropped from 14.8 percent in the freshman class of 1972 to 13.0 percent in the current freshman class.
>
> The data on the financial and racial backgrounds of this year's entering students are contained in a report entitled "The American Freshman: National Norms for Fall 1973."
>
> . . . Commenting on the decline in minority enrollment, Lawrence V

Barclay, director of minority affairs for the College Entrance Examination Board, said, "The survey confirms what I had suspected."

Last spring, Mr. Barclay participated in a conference at Oberlin College at which admissions and financial aid representatives of many institutions warned that colleges and universities were backing off from their earlier determination to increase nonwhite enrollments.

As a college education has become more expensive and inflation has chipped at family budgets, middle-income students have been competing more vigorously with low-income students for the limited amount of available aid.

Students from families with incomes of less than $6,000 made up 14.1 percent of the freshman class of 1972 and only 11.1 percent in 1973. At the other end of the scale, students from families with incomes of $30,000 or more made up 9.1 percent of the 1972 freshmen and 11.2 percent in 1973.

William Boyd, executive director of the Educational Policy Center, a nonprofit organization in New York City that studies minority opportunities in education, sees students from poor families losing out as financial aid officers are reallocating funds to the benefit of the middle-class.

Are families and students paying more or less of the cost of higher education than they once did?

The answer is that, on the average, they are paying less. Measured in constant dollars, monetary outlays by families per student are about what they were in 1929-30; but subsidies (mostly public) per student have nearly tripled. (See Table 7 in *Higher Education: Who Pays? Who Benefits? Who Should Pay?,* reproduced as Table 10 in the Statistical Appendix). Average family outlays per student were once about 40 percent higher than average public subsidies per student (again in constant dollars). By 1969-70, they were about 20 percent less. Generally what has happened is that the real cost to the family has remained about the same for almost 40 years even as family real income has increased substantially–in fact, more than doubled. Real costs per student (including public subsidies), however, have risen, and this extra burden of real costs has been absorbed by subsidies. Relatively more of the subsidies, also, are now public and less of them come proportionately from private philanthropy.[2] Greater outside support has been necessary, and it has come mostly from taxpayers (see Chart 9).

[2]The data in Table 10, when analyzed, are not inconsistent with those in Table 3, which show a gradual rise in both public and private tuition over the years since 1929-30. However, the overall rise in tuition has been more moderate than in either public or private tuition, because the proportion of total enrollment in the comparatively low-tuition public sector has greatly increased. In addition, tuition has increased at a more rapid rate over the period since 1929-30 than have subsistence costs, reflecting the fact that costs of higher education have risen more rapidly than the consumer price index.

CHART 9 Rise in real cost per student (a) to family and (b) to non-family subsidies, 1929-30 to 1969-70

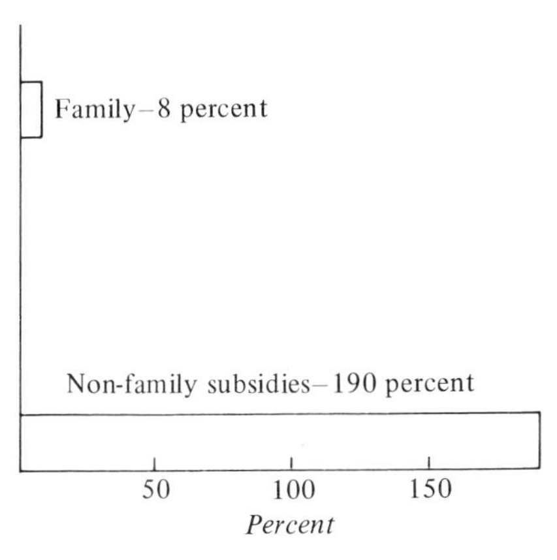

SOURCE: Table 10

This does not mean, of course, that all families with college-age children have been affected alike by these trends. The relative increase in the role of public subsidies reflects in large part the increase in the share of total enrollment in comparatively low-tuition public institutions. It also reflects a pronounced increase in federal student aid, with veterans' benefits playing an especially important role in recent years. Families in the "upper-middle" and "upper" income groups, with children in private colleges and universities, have always met a high share of total costs.

Are private institutions under competitive pressure from public institutions?

The answer is in the affirmative, but the situation varies greatly from category to category and from institution to institution. The four-year institutions under the greatest pressure are the "comprehensive colleges and universities" and the "liberal arts colleges II" (the less selective liberal arts colleges). See Table 2. The private two-year institutions are also under substantial pressure. The competitive disadvantage in attracting students is greatest for private institutions when the ratio is largest. (See Chart 10).

How important is tuition?

The cost for a student attending college is comprised of four main components: tuition and fees, room and board, other expenses, and foregone income beyond the cost of subsistence.[3] For public and private four-year institutions, a generalized distribution of costs is about as follows:

	Public		*Private*	
	Amount	*Percent*	*Amount*	*Percent*
Tuition and fees	$ 500*	9	$2,200*	31
Board and room	$1,100*	21	$1,300*	19
Other expenses	$ 600	11	$ 600	9
Foregone income (net of student subsistence)	$3,100+	59	$2,900+	41
	$5,300	100	$7,000	100

*Estimated from data in U.S. National Center for Educational Statistics (1973, p. 113).

+Foregone income (net of student subsistence) is lower in private than in public institutions, because board and room charges tend to be higher in private institutions.

Thus tuition is an important, but not the most important, element of cost—it is *a* cost, not *the* cost of college attendance. Private tuition at four or more times the rate of public tuition may raise total costs at the private institution not by four times but by more like about 32 percent above that at a public institution. This is, of course, a substantial difference; but, if higher educational costs at private institutions (15 percent) reflect equivalent higher quality, then the significance of the difference diminishes substantially. For greater detail see Table 11.

Also, an average tuition rise equal to 1 percent of educational costs (over and above the current ratio of tuition to cost) at a representative public institution will add about four-tenths of 1 percent to total costs ($20 on $5,200); and would add about 4 percent if continued over a ten-year period. The potential impacts of a "modest and gradual rise in public as against private tuition" have thus been exaggerated in some recent discussions.

Will tax policy by itself be sufficient to redistribute equality of educational opportunity?

It is most unlikely. Yet it has been suggested recently that taxes are the best way to accomplish this. (1) Tax policy has not accomplished this task in the past nor are revisions likely in the foreseeable future which

[3]Including foregone income *plus* the cost of subsistence would involve double counting, because young earners must typically meet the cost of subsistence from their earnings.

CHART 10 Ratios of private to public tuition and required fees as a percentage of educational costs, 1971-72*

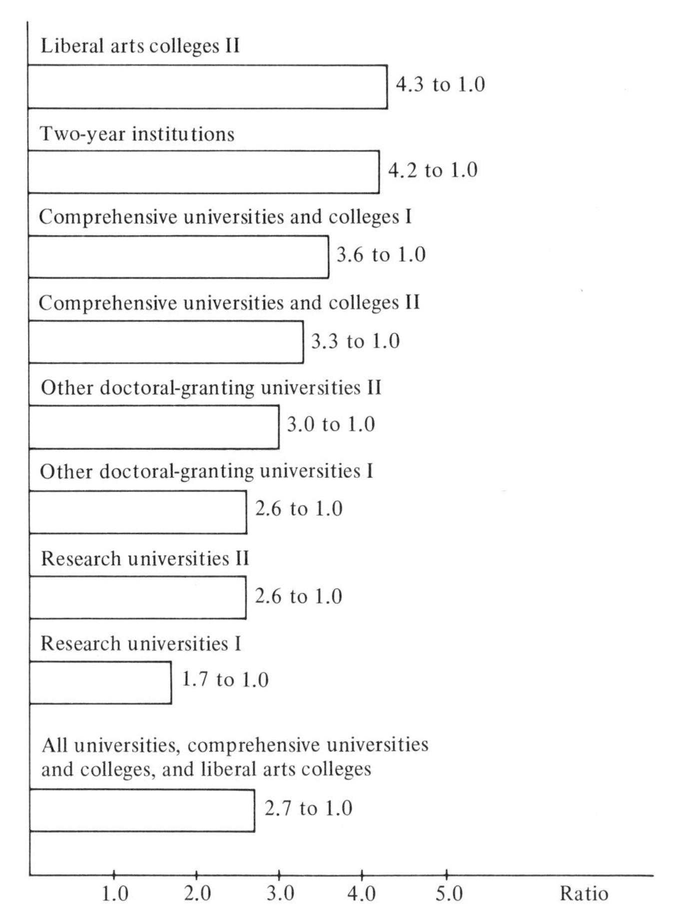

*Data for Liberal Arts Colleges I are not included, because there are only two public institutions in that category.

SOURCE: Table 2.

could accomplish it. (2) Even in theory, expenditures from taxes are important as well as receipts from taxes. It is *fiscal policy,* including both source of funds and use of funds, that is involved. Funds can be expended, just as they can be collected, in progressive, regressive or proportional ways. Student subsidies, whether by tuition below cost or by direct aid, are a form of expenditure of tax revenues and cannot be neglected in favor of sole concern for tax receipts. (3) Nor could tax policy, by itself, provide for equality of opportunity in areas of higher education. This requires specific expenditure policy as well.

The overall financing of higher education does now have an impact on the distribution of opportunity, as we have seen. It will continue to have an impact. Higher education cannot escape some responsibility by directing attention solely to tax policy. Both tax policy and expenditure policy, over which higher education holds some direct and indirect influence, are important.

8. Equity—an Elusive Goal

Achieving equity in tuition policy involves many complexities:

- Equity between low-income and high-income students. The Commission recommended comparatively more subsidy for low- and middle-income students. This also relates to opportunities for minority youth as compared with majority youth.
- Equity between family and public support. The Commission recommended more public support in the short run, particularly to finance greater equality of opportunity.
- Equity between state and federal support. The Commission recommended a modest redistribution from the states to the federal government.
- Equity between public and private institutions. The Commission recommended (a) immediate public support for private colleges in all 50 states and (b) a "modest and gradual" increase in tuition in public four-year institutions, which would incidentally result in a gradual narrowing of the current tuition gap.
- Equity among public institutions. Table 4 shows great discrepancies among public institutions in the same state. The most likely way to eliminate some of these inequities is by raising tuition at some institutions while holding it even at others, and, in the process, raising the average level.
- Equity among private institutions, when public support is made available, as between the heavily endowed and the non-endowed.
- Equity among levels of instruction. Lower-division students now pay more of their educational costs in four-year institutions than do upper-division students, and undergraduates pay more of these costs than do graduate students.

- Equity among "full" users and "partial" users and non-users. Table 12 shows that in 1970 about 62 percent of all persons were non-users of higher education; about 13 percent were "partial" users either now or in the past or potentially in the future in the sense that they did or had or would attend private institutions which receive some direct or indirect public subsidies; about 25 percent were "full users" in the sense that they did or had or would attend a public institution of higher education. Everybody, of course, is a user of higher education in the broader sense that the social benefits are widely distributed, but the degree of direct private benefit varies considerably.

Viewing all of these considerations, one might almost be led to agree with Emerson that "one man's justice is another's injustice."

The Commission concluded that no "equal and exact" justice is possible, but that some reasonable adjustments could be made which would bring greater equity. The tasks of those at the state and institutional level working on tuition policy are most complex and call for the best and most balanced of judgment in each individual situation. And many situations will have elements which do currently and may in the future lead to quite different solutions than any general guideline may imply.

Situations vary, and solutions will and should vary. Suggested guidelines may, however, still be helpful as one aspect of decision-making. Justice, in this as in other areas, is still "the art of the good and the fair," as the Latin saying went.

9. Additional Comments

(1) Tuition is now rising rapidly in some public institutions. As we have seen, it rose 15 percent for lower-division students and 30 percent for upper-division students in the current academic year at the University of Michigan. A suggestion which looks like a series of rising hills to some in the current year, may shortly look like a welcome plateau even to the same persons. Howard Bowen has said: "The Carnegie report is quite moderate and generally favors a continuation of the present system of finance rather than an abrupt change," and then added that "the recommendations of the Carnegie Commission are already becoming a reality."[1] As a consequence, some of the antagonists of today may become the protagonists of tomorrow. Bowen has also said: ". . . I am in general agreement with the main thrust of the Carnegie report. Indeed, about a year ago I reached essentially the same position in my ERIC paper *Who Benefits from Higher Education and Who Should Pay?"* (See Attachment B for his full statement).

(2) The proposed increases in the total sum available for Basic Opportunity Grants—from $122 million in fiscal 1973 to $475 million in fiscal 1974 and to $1.3 billion in fiscal 1975 (*Chronicle of Higher Education,* February 14, 1974, p. 4), if fully funded and followed by further increases in subsequent years, will greatly ease financial burdens for students from families with incomes up to about the $12,000 level and to the $18,000 level under exceptional circumstances; that is to say, for families in the lower range of the "middle-middle" income group and below and rising into the "upper-middle" income group. The ceiling on amounts of assistance should be raised, as the Commission earlier recommended, "in line with increases in educational and subsistence costs." It might even rise to cover many in the "upper-middle" income group. This would not be very costly,[2] and may be both necessary and

[1]See Bowen (1974).

[2]National Commission on the Financing of Postsecondary Education (1973, pp. 315-316).

desirable on other grounds.

There has been a quite legitimate fear that tuition might rise while student aid remained stable. Actually, proposed funds for the Basic Opportunity Grants program of student aid (increasingly the most important one) would mean a rise at a faster rate than any contemplated or even remotely possible rise in tuition rates.

The Basic Opportunity Grants program does make allowance for tuition costs in calculating need. This opens up one way of shifting costs from the state to the federal level. And eligibility standards will determine how high up in the "middle class" aid may be given. This is up to Congress and the President. The basic legislation is in existence.

Targeted subsidies to students in need are both a more certain and a less expensive method of assuring more equal access than across-the-board reductions in tuition, as the National Commission on the Financing of Postsecondary Education has noted.[3] More can be done with the same amount of money.

The best current prospect for improving access to higher education is full funding of, and other improvements in, the Basic Opportunity Grants program, and adequate funding of the State Incentive Grants program provided for in the Higher Education Amendments of 1972.

While the prospects for increasing student aid now seem to be most favorable, the Commission would wish to repeat its strongly held conviction: *"We are opposed to any increase in tuition at public institutions except as such increases are offset by the availability of student aid for lower-income students."*

(3) Any financial plan, as the Commission earlier noted, should be considered "interim." Many changes are taking place. The most sudden and basic one may come, if, and when, some court rules that a needs test must apply to the income of an individual aged 18 or over and not to the income of his or her family. But many other changes are also either likely or inevitable, and some reasonable flexibility of approach in response to a changing environment may be the course of wisdom; rigidity of position can build up unsupportable tensions and consequences.

Sober reflection, careful analysis of the facts, and a broad consideration for the general welfare of higher education and of the nation should lead to some sensible conclusions about a difficult set of circumstances, and to a reasonable consensus among legislative leaders and those drawn from public and private higher education.

[3] *Ibid.*, particularly pp. 310-311.

Statistical Appendix

CHART A Distribution of total subsidy funds benefiting undergraduates, by family income quintile, under four alternative assumptions

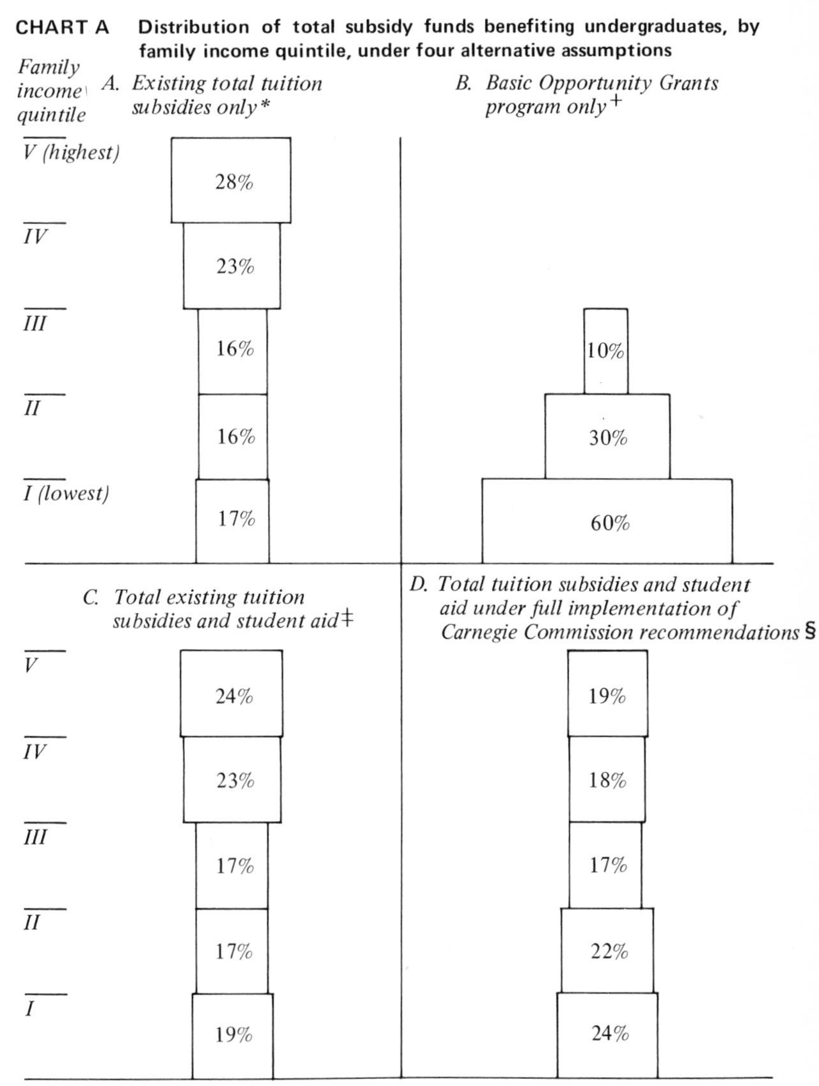

*Includes total tuition subsidies at public and private institutions.

+Estimated on same basis as in Chart 3.

‡Includes total tuition subsidies and student aid at public and private institutions.

§ Includes total tuition subsidies and student aid at public and private institutions, including increases in student aid and modifications in tuition subsidies recommended by the Carnegie Commission.

SOURCES: Estimated by Carnegie Commission staff from U.S. Office of Education, U.S. Bureau of the Census, and California State Scholarship and Loan Commission data.

NOTE: In both Chart 3 and Chart A, student aid estimates based on California State Scholarship and Loan Commission data have been adjusted to exclude aid to graduate students, to include only subsidized interest costs of loans, and to link family income distributions to nationwide undergraduate enrollment data.

TABLE 1 Estimated public expenditures for student aid under Carnegie Commission recommendations,* 1973-74 (in millions of dollars)

Program	*1973-74*
Federal	
Basic opportunity grants	$2,000
Federal cost of State Incentive grants	120
Work-study program	970
Graduate talent search	15
Doctoral fellowships	80
Counseling program	30
Subtotal	3,215
State	
Scholarship and other student aid programs	360
TOTAL	$3,575

*Does not include veterans' benefits, social security benefits, interest on loans, or expenditures under certain other miscellaneous federal programs. Veterans' benefits and social security benefits are omitted, because large proportions of these benefits are expended for subsistence and thus do not affect the relationship between total tuition subsidies and student aid (see Chart 2) with which we are here particularly concerned. In addition, veterans' benefits may be expected to decline in future years as Vietnam veterans complete their education. Interest on loans (and the cost of defaults) are omitted, because the National Student Loan Program that the Commission has recommended differs so substantially from the present Guaranteed Loan Program that relative costs of the two programs are not comparable.

SOURCES: Adapted by Carnegie Commission staff from estimates originally presented in Carnegie Commission (1970, pp. 32-33; 1972, p. 94; and 1973*b*, pp. 121-122).

TABLE 2 **Revenue from tuition and other required fees as a percentage of educational expenditures, by type and control of institution, United States, 1971-72***

	Tuition as a percentage of educational expenditures		
	Public	*Private*	*Ratio*
Universities	23.1	47.0	2.0:1
Research universities I	20.9	35.6	1.7:1
Research universities II	24.6	64.6	2.6:1
Other doctoral-granting universities I	25.9	67.0	2.6:1
Other doctoral-granting universities II	26.2	78.9	3.0:1
Comprehensive colleges and universities	22.8	81.0	3.6:1
Comprehensive colleges and universities I	22.4	80.6	3.6:1
Comprehensive colleges and universities II	25.3	82.7	3.3:1
Liberal arts colleges	19.5	73.1	3.7:1
Liberal arts colleges I	+	74.8	
Liberal arts colleges II	16.7	72.1	4.3:1
Two-year institutions	16.7	70.3	4.2:1
All universities, comprehensive colleges, and liberal arts colleges	22.9	61.9	2.7:1

*Educational expenditures include those expenditures classified by the U.S. Office of Education under "educational and general expenses," except for organized research. For further details, see footnote 2, page 4. Specialized institutions and institutions not reporting financial data are excluded.

+There are only two public institutions in this category.

SOURCE: Adapted from U.S. Office of Education data by Carnegie Commission staff.

TABLE 3 Average annual gross tuition and required fees, and per capita disposable personal income, public and private colleges and universities, 1929-30 to 1973-74 (in constant dollars)

	*Public tuition**		*Private tuition**			*Per capita income+*	
ar	*Amount*	*Annual average rate of change*	*Amount*	*Annual average rate of change*	*Ratio, private to public tuition*	*Amount*	*Annual average rate of change*
29-30	$125		$447		3.6	$1,182	
33-34	165	7.2	575	6.5	3.5	923	-6.0
37-38	164	-0.2	535	-1.7	3.3	1,146	5.6
41-42	168	0.6	540	0.2	3.2	1,504	7.0
45-46	162	-1.0	486	-2.6	3.0	1,624	1.9
49-50	247	11.1	579	4.5	2.3	1,597	-0.6
53-54	173	-8.5	578	-0.1	3.3	1,720	1.9
57-58	190	2.4	683	4.3	3.6	1,838	1.7
61-62	215	3.1	884	6.7	4.1	1,940	1.4
65-66	251	3.9	1,090	5.4	4.3	2,287	4.2
69-70	283	3.0	1,341	5.3	4.7	2,565	2.9
73-74	305‡	1.9	1,514‡	3.1	5.0	2,928‡	3.4
29-30 1973-74		2.0		2.8			2.1

*O'Neill data, used for the years 1929-30 to 1965-66, represent gross tuition and fee income per full-time-equivalent student; U.S. Office of Education data, used for the years 1969-70 to 1973-74, represent average tuition and fee charges per full-time undergraduate student (in the case of public institutions, for state residents).

+Average per capita income for two adjacent calendar years.

‡Estimated.

SOURCES: O'Neill (1973, p. 44); U.S. National Center for Educational Statistics (1972, p. 107, and 1973, p. 113); and U.S. President (1972, p. 213 and 1974, p. 269).

TABLE 4 Revenue from tuition and other required fees as percentage of educational expenditures,* by state and type of institution, public institutions, United States, 1971-72+

State	*Universities*		*Comprehensive universities and colleges*		*Liberal arts colleges*		*Two-year institutions*	
Alabama	22.1%	(2)	19.8%	(9)	25.4%	(1)	21.2%	(14)
Alaska	9.5	(1)						
Arizona	23.6	(2)	22.2	(1)			6.2	(11)
Arkansas	22.7	(1)	30.3	(8)			22.7	(3)
California	20.1	(7)	13.5	(16)	16.8	(4)	2.5	(87)
Colorado	35.1	(3)	28.9	(7)			16.2	(10)
Connecticut	14.1	(1)	33.1	(4)			17.4	(16)
Delaware	27.0	(11)	22.6	(1)			15.8	(2)
District of Columbia			4.6	(1)			3.5	(1)
Florida	15.4	(2)	21.7	(5)			23.2	(24)
Georgia	16.4	(3)	27.7	(12)			30.2	(13)
Hawaii	12.3	(1)	8.3	(1)			5.8	(6)
Idaho	10.9	(1)	9.1	(3)			18.6	(2)
Illinois	16.2	(4)	22.3	(7)	11.7	(1)	15.0	(42)
Indiana	27.7	(3)	29.7	(5)			35.0	(14)
Iowa	18.4	(2)	30.2	(1)			23.6	(16)
Kansas	20.5	(2)	25.6	(1)			18.4	(20)
Kentucky	17.3	(2)	16.1	(3)			39.0	(1)
Louisiana	23.6	(1)	19.2	(11)			11.4	(6)
Maine	27.3	(1)					16.9	(1)
Maryland	32.6	(1)	20.5	(6)	20.1	(3)	24.3	(12)
Massachusetts	28.5	(1)	16.0	(10)	9.2	(1)	22.9	(12)
Michigan	28.2	(4)	29.7	(10)	22.8	(1)	26.5	(27)
Minnesota	14.6	(1)	26.2	(8)			23.7	(20)
Mississippi	28.8	(4)	28.0	(5)			15.2	(15)
Missouri	22.2	(3)	27.6	(8)	21.4	(1)	26.0	(14)
Montana	23.0	(2)	19.0	(3)			15.9	(3)
Nebraska	17.6	(1)	44.9	(5)			18.1	(8)
Nevada	19.9	(1)	23.5	(1)				
New Hampshire	43.7	(1)	61.8	(2)			17.6	(1)
New Jersey	17.6	(1)	29.2	(9)			28.1	(11)
New Mexico	14.8	(2)	21.1	(3)			31.7	(8)
New York							24.3	(39)
CUNY	10.9	(1)	15.4	(6)	‡			
SUNY	17.5	(3)	26.7	(10)	‡			
North Carolina	14.1	(2)	23.4	(9)	20.0	(1)	7.5	(34)
North Dakota	22.7	(2)	31.5	(3)	21.5	(1)	28.7	(5)
Ohio	42.2	(7)	46.5	(5)			39.2	(33)
Oklahoma	28.8	(2)	31.0	(9)	22.0	(1)	27.1	(14)
Oregon	26.4	(2)	27.5	(4)			19.4	(13)
Pennsylvania	32.8	(3)	36.3	(11)			37.0	(20)
Rhode Island	33.4	(1)	28.9	(1)			20.9	(1)
South Carolina	19.0	(2)	16.2	(3)	37.6	(3)	24.0	(22)
South Dakota	22.7	(1)	24.1	(5)				
Tennessee	30.0	(1)	26.1	(9)			14.5	(8)

TABLE 4 (cont.)

State	*Universities*		*Comprehensive universities and colleges*		*Liberal arts colleges*		*Two-year institutions*	
Texas	8.0%	(7)	14.3%	(12)			17.7%	(44)
Utah	21.2	(2)	23.6	(2)			26.6	(1)
Vermont	41.7	(1)	54.7	(1)	48.6%	(2)	22.2	(1)
Virginia			32.2	(8)	51.5	(1)	21.0	(19)
Washington	14.2	(2)	18.5	(4)			13.4	(21)
West Virginia	20.7	(1)	5.9	(9)			23.1	(5)
Wisconsin	29.3	(1)	27.2	(7)			6.8	(20)
Wyoming	20.4	(1)					13.2	(4)
Outlying areas			8.9	(3)	7.5	(1)		

*Includes instruction and departmental research; extension and public service; libraries; general administration, general institutional expense, and student services; organized activities relating to educational departments; other sponsored programs; and all other educational and general expense. Excludes expenditures for organized research. Numbers in parentheses represent number of institutions (or in some cases campuses) reporting.

+Includes United States and outlying areas; excludes institutions that did not report financial data; specialized institutions are excluded.

‡Insufficient data available.

SOURCE: Adapted from U.S. Office of Education data by the Carnegie Commission staff. For a description of the Carnegie Commission classification of institutions used here, see Carnegie Commission (1973*a*). We are indebted to budget analysts at the State University of New York and at the University of Massachusetts for supplying data to correct apparent errors or omissions relating to their institutions.

TABLE 5 **Revenue from tuition and other required fees as a percentage of educational expenditures, land-grant universities and colleges, by state, 1971-72**

State and institution	*Percentage*
Alabama	
Alabama A & M University	18.5
Auburn University	19.7
Alaska	
*University of Alaska**	9.5
Arizona	
University of Arizona	19.4
Arkansas	
University of Arkansas	22.7
University of Arkansas, Pine Bluff	19.3
California	
University of California, Berkeley	27.2
Colorado	
Colorado State University	33.3

TABLE 5 (cont.)

State and institution	*Percentage*
Connecticut	
University of Connecticut	14.1
Delaware	
Delaware State College	22.6
University of Delaware	27.0
District of Columbia	
Federal City College	4.6
Florida	
Florida A & M University	17.1
University of Florida	13.2
Georgia	
Fort Valley State College	19.6
University of Georgia	16.7
Guam	
University of Guam	7.8
Hawaii	
University of Hawaii	13.0
Idaho	
University of Idaho	10.9
Illinois	
University of Illinois	13.7
Indiana	
Purdue University	20.9
Iowa	
Iowa State University	29.5
Kansas	
Kansas State University	21.8
Kentucky	
Kentucky State University	NA
University of Kentucky	11.2
Louisiana	
Louisiana State University	23.6
Southern University	16.2
Maine	
*University of Maine**	27.3
Maryland	
University of Maryland	32.6
Massachusetts	
Massachusetts Institute of Technology	35.0
University of Massachusetts	28.7

TABLE 5 (cont.)

State and institution	*Percentage*
Michigan	
Michigan State University	26.7
Minnesota	
University of Minnesota	14.6
Mississippi	
Alcorn A & M College	25.3
Mississippi State University	20.0
Missouri	
Lincoln University	19.7
University of Missouri	21.4
Montana	
Montana State University	21.7
Nebraska	
University of Nebraska	17.6
Nevada	
University of Nevada	19.9
New Hampshire	
University of New Hampshire	43.7
New Jersey	
Rutgers, The State University of New Jersey	17.6
New Mexico	
New Mexico State University	16.3
New York	
Cornell University	31.4
North Carolina	
North Carolina A & T State University	NA
*North Carolina State University**	13.4
North Dakota	
North Dakota State University	23.6
Ohio	
Ohio State University	35.2
Oklahoma	
Langston University	31.8
Oklahoma State University	29.6
Oregon	
Oregon State University	26.7
Pennsylvania	
*Pennsylvania State University**	35.4
Puerto Rico	
*University of Puerto Rico**	8.4

TABLE 5 (cont.)

State and institution	*Percentage*
Rhode Island	
University of Rhode Island	33.4
South Carolina	
Clemson University	16.5
South Carolina State College	3.7
South Dakota	
South Dakota State University	23.1
Tennessee	
Tennessee State University	23.7
University of Tennessee	30.0
Texas	
Prairie View A & M College	8.2
Texas A & M University	3.7
Utah	
Utah State University	21.9
Vermont	
University of Vermont	41.7
Virgin Islands	
College of the Virgin Islands	7.5
Virginia	
Virginia Polytechnic Institute and State University	NA
Virginia State College	22.6
Washington	
Washington State University	12.8
West Virginia	
West Virginia University	20.7
Wisconsin	
University of Wisconsin	29.3
Wyoming	
University of Wyoming	20.4

*Includes tuition and required fees and educational costs for more than one campus of the institution; unless otherwise noted, percentages are for the main campus of the institution.

NOTE: NA indicates that financial data were not available for this institution for 1971-72.

SOURCE: Adapted from U.S. Office of Education data by Carnegie Commission staff.

TABLE 6 Undergraduate tuition and required fees for state residents, public four-year institutions, by state and type of institution,* 1971-72 to 1973-74

State and type of institution	*1971-72+*	*1972-73+*	*1973-74+*	*Percentage change, 1971-72 to 1973-74 (top of range)*
Alabama				
Auburn University	$450	$450	$525	17
University of Alabama, main campus	510	510	510	0
Comprehensive universities and colleges	330-579	330-579	330-579	0
Alaska				
University of Alaska, main campus	322	402	472	47
Arizona				
Arizona State University	320	320	320	0
University of Arizona	350	411	411	17
Comprehensive universities and colleges (Northern Arizona University)	304	304	330	9
Arkansas				
University of Arkansas, main campus	375	400	400	7
Comprehensive universities and colleges	300-410	400-410	400-410	0
California				
University of California	640	644	644	1
Comprehensive universities and colleges	117-164	160-168	160-168	2
Liberal arts colleges (excluding University of California, Santa Cruz)	§	117-157	117-157	§
Colorado				
Colorado State University	567	570	778	37
University of Colorado, Boulder	552	576	593	7
University of Northern Colorado	390	402	427	9
Comprehensive universities and colleges	318-459	333-462	330-474	3
Connecticut				
University of Connecticut	655	655	715	9
Comprehensive universities and colleges	222-570	450-570	450-570	0

TABLE 6 (cont.)

State and type of institution	*1971-72+*	*1972-73+*	*1973-74+*	*Percentage change, 1971-72 to 1973-74 (top of range)*
Delaware				
University of Delaware	$425	$475	$585	38
Comprehensive universities and colleges (Delaware State College)	325	345	355	9
District of Columbia				
Comprehensive universities and colleges (Federal City College)	132	132	132	0
Florida				
Florida State University	570	570	570	0
University of Florida	570	570	570	0
Comprehensive universities and colleges	570	570	570	0
Georgia				
Georgia Institute of Technology	504	534	534	6
University of Georgia	485	519	539	11
Comprehensive universities and colleges	315-405	345-435	367-435	7
Hawaii				
University of Hawaii, Manoa	233	233	223	-4
Idaho				
University of Idaho	346	356	380	10
Comprehensive universities and colleges	§	240-373	240-376	§
Illinois				
Illinois State University	531	585	611	15
Northern Illinois University	568	574	603	6
Southern Illinois University, Carbondale	564	579	579	3
University of Illinois, Urbana-Champaign	558	686	686	23
Comprehensive universities and colleges	396-592	520-692	476-599	1
Liberal arts colleges (Sangamon State University)	447	447	472	6

TABLE 6 (cont.)

State and type of institution	*1971-72+*	*1972-73+*	*1973-74+*	*Percentage change, 1971-72 to 1973-74 (top of range)*
Indiana				
Ball State University	$540	$630	$630	17
Indiana University	650	650	682	5
Purdue University	700	700	700	0
Comprehensive universities and colleges (Indiana State University)	574	600	660	15
Iowa				
Iowa State University	600	600	600	0
University of Iowa	620	620	620	0
Comprehensive universities and colleges (University of Northern Iowa)	600	600	600	0
Kansas				
Kansas State University	476	476	526	11
University of Kansas	466	486	544	17
Comprehensive universities and colleges	382-449	386-459	390-536	19
Kentucky				
University of Kentucky	330	405	480	45
Comprehensive universities and colleges	300-360	360-380	420-425	18
Louisiana				
Louisiana State University, main campus	320	320	320	0
Comprehensive universities and colleges	270-318	270-326	274-334	5
Maine				
University of Maine, main campus	562	562	562	0
Comprehensive universities and colleges	400-466	400	400	-14
Liberal arts colleges	§	400-430	400-430	§
Maryland				
University of Maryland, main campus	599	639	698	17
Comprehensive universities and colleges	200-415	335-721	520-721	74
Liberal arts colleges	442-589	460-500	470-560	-5

TABLE 6 (cont.)

State and type of institution	*1971-72*+	*1972-73*+	*1973-74*+	*Percentage change, 1971-72 to 1973-74 (top of range)*
Massachusetts				
University of Massachusetts, main campus	$412	$469	$520	26
Comprehensive universities and colleges	200-324	250-382	300-420	30
Michigan				
Michigan State University	630	675	720	14
University of Michigan	660	696	800-904‡	37
Wayne State University	618	668	704	14
Western Michigan University	558	558	558	0
Comprehensive universities and colleges	450-512	450-565	495-602	18
Minnesota				
University of Minnesota, main campus	600	641	683	14
Comprehensive universities and colleges	§	307-438	333-477	§
Mississippi				
Mississippi State University	492	506	506	3
University of Mississippi	506	516	516	2
University of Southern Mississippi	477	477	477	0
Comprehensive universities and colleges	350-465	399-465	400-474	2
Missouri				
University of Missouri	500	540	540	8
Comprehensive universities and colleges	250-310	250-300	250-315	2
Liberal arts colleges (Missouri Western State College)	340	340	340	0
Montana				
Montana State University	471	471	476	1
University of Montana	471	471	487	3
Comprehensive universities and colleges	§	413-445	430-450	§
Nebraska				
University of Nebraska, main campus	534	534	534	0
Comprehensive universities and colleges	413-423	403-443	§	§

TABLE 6 (cont.)

State and type of institution	*1971-72+*	*1972-73+*	*1973-74+*	*Percentage change, 1971-72 to 1973-74 (top of range)*
Nevada				
University of Nevada, main campus	$519	$519	$519	0
Comprehensive universities and colleges (University of Nevada, Las Vegas)	532	532	532	0
New Hampshire				
University of New Hampshire	1,084	1,034	984	-9
Comprehensive universities and colleges	724-758	714-733	714-733	-3
New Jersey				
Rutgers University, main campus	470	655	725	54
Comprehensive universities and colleges	350-500	636-679	636-709	42
New Mexico				
New Mexico State University	466	466	466	0
University of New Mexico	431	456	456	6
Comprehensive universities and colleges (Western New Mexico University)	166	333	333	101
New York				
State University of New York, university campuses	575	740-890‡	750-900‡	57
Comprehensive universities and colleges				
CUNY, Queens College	§	138	138	§
SUNY, college campuses	640-890	650-895‡	650-895‡	1
Liberal arts colleges	625-645	745-895	650-800	24
North Carolina				
North Carolina State University, main campus	427	427	474	11
University of North Carolina, main campus	402	422	439	9
Comprehensive universities and colleges	§	§	368-507	§

TABLE 6 (cont.)

State and type of institution	*1971-72+*	*1972-73+*	*1973-74+*	*Percentage change, 1971-72 to 1973-74 (top of range)*
North Dakota				
North Dakota State University	$435	$435	$435	0
University of North Dakota, main campus	456	456	456	0
Comprehensive universities and colleges	396-406	396-406	400-415	2
Liberal arts colleges (Mayville State College)	399	399	399	0
Ohio				
Kent State University	732	804	804	10
Miami University	750	780	780	4
Ohio State University	720	750	750	4
Comprehensive universities and colleges	§	570-780	630-780	§
Oklahoma				
Oklahoma State University	476	484	484	2
University of Oklahoma	448	448	448	0
Comprehensive universities and colleges	315-356	327-355	332-355	0
Liberal arts colleges (Oklahoma College of Liberal Arts)	§	335	335	§
Oregon				
Oregon State University	498	506	536	8
University of Oregon	528	534	566	7
Comprehensive universities and colleges	513-519	513-519	549	6
Pennsylvania				
Pennsylvania State University	780	885	900	15
Temple University	970	970	1,050	8
University of Pittsburgh	982	982	1,012	3
Comprehensive universities and colleges (excluding Lincoln University)	662-788	700-790	415-840	7
Rhode Island				
University of Rhode Island	761	761	761	0
Comprehensive universities and colleges (Rhode Island College)	490	490	490	0

TABLE 6 (cont.)

State and type of institution	*1971-72+*	*1972-73+*	*1973-74+*	*Percentage change, 1971-72 to 1973-74 (top of range)*
South Carolina				
Clemson University	$640	$640	$640	0
University of South Carolina	550	570	570	4
Comprehensive universities and colleges (Winthrop College)	520	520	520	0
Liberal arts colleges (Francis Marion College)	410	410	410	0
South Dakota				
University of South Dakota	468	500	554	18
Comprehensive universities and colleges	§	345-488	397-550	§
Tennessee				
University of Tennessee, main campus	378	399	399	6
Comprehensive universities and colleges	318-396	318-396	318-416	5
Texas				
East Texas State University	250	250	322	29
North Texas State University	126	152	170	35
Texas A & M University	262	279	288	10
Texas Technical University	252	290	292	16
University of Houston	280	290	290	4
University of Texas, Austin	262	267	378	44
Comprehensive universities and colleges	226-280	120-284	120-300	7
Utah				
University of Utah	480	480	480	0
Utah State University	438	438	453	3
Comprehensive universities and colleges (Weber State College)	405	405	405	0
Vermont				
University of Vermont	1,078	1,086	1,088	1
Comprehensive universities and colleges (Castleton State College)	788	720	720	-9
Liberal arts colleges	§	720	720	§

TABLE 6 (cont.)

State and type of institution	*1971-72+*	*1972-73+*	*1973-74+*	*Percentage change, 1971-72 to 1973-74 (top of range)*
Virginia				
University of Virginia, main campus	$542	$597	$622	15
Virginia Commonwealth University	§	540	590	§
Virginia Polytechnic Institute and State University	597	627	627	5
Comprehensive universities and colleges	414-647	462-647	470-690	7
Liberal arts colleges (University of Virginia, Mary Washington College)	§	762	792	§
Washington				
University of Washington	495	564	564	14
Washington State University	495	564	564	14
Comprehensive universities and colleges	495	495	495	0
West Virginia				
West Virginia University	292	310	310	6
Comprehensive universities and colleges	116-282	232-282	240-282	0
Wisconsin				
University of Wisconsin, Madison and Milwaukee	550	558	573-628‡	14
Comprehensive universities and colleges	460-544	518-544	519-627‡	15
Wyoming				
University of Wyoming	391	411	411	5

*Institutions are classified in accordance with the Carnegie Commission Classification (Carnegie Commission, 1973*a*). All universities listed by name are classified as research universities or doctoral-granting universities in that classification. There are a few omissions because of absence of data. Under comprehensive universities and colleges and under liberal arts colleges, the name of the institution is included in parentheses if the data relate to only one institution (or campus).

+Where the charge reported for the preceding year differs from the charge originally reported for that year, we have used the more recently reported figure.

‡The lower figure applies to lower-division students; the higher figure applies to upper-division students. In the SUNY colleges and among comprehensive universities and colleges in Wisconsin, the charges vary somewhat from college to college, and the lower figure is usually the smallest charge applicable to lower-division students, while the higher figure is the largest charge applicable to upper-division students.

§ Comparable data not available.

SOURCES: National Association of State Universities and Land-Grant Colleges (annual); and American Association of State Universities and Colleges (annual). We are indebted to staff members of these organizations for assistance in overcoming apparent inconsistencies in the data.

TABLE 7 Undergraduate tuition and required fees for nonresidents, public four-year institutions, by state and type of institution,* 1971-72 to 1973-74

State and type of institution	*1971-72+*	*1972-73+*	*1973-74+*	*Percentage change, 1971-72 to 1973-74 (top of range)*
Alabama				
Auburn University	$ 900	$ 900	$1,050	17
University of Alabama, main campus	1,020	1,020	1,020	0
Comprehensive universities and colleges	540-1,050	450-1,050	470-1,050	0
Alaska				
University of Alaska, main campus	922	1,002	1,072	16
Arizona				
Arizona State University	1,210	1,210	1,210	0
University of Arizona	1,240	1,301	1,301	5
Comprehensive universities and colleges (Northern Arizona University)	969	969	995	3
Arkansas				
University of Arkansas, main campus	905	930	930	3
Comprehensive universities and colleges	670-940	680-940	680-940	0
California				
University of California	2,140	2,144	2,144	0
Comprehensive universities and colleges	1,110-1,277	1,110-1,278	716-1,399	10
Liberal arts colleges (excluding University of California, Santa Cruz)	§	1,100-1,270	1,100-1,270	§
Colorado				
Colorado State University	1,796	1,759	1,895	6
University of Colorado, Boulder	1,820	1,895	1,959	8
University of Northern Colorado	840	1,200	1,303	55
Comprehensive universities and colleges	868-1,389	1,062-1,431	1,003-1,489	7
Connecticut				
University of Connecticut	1,555	1,555	1,715	10
Comprehensive universities and colleges	800-1,350	1,210-1,422	1,350-1,424	5

TABLE 7 (cont.)

State and type of institution	*1971-72+*	*1972-73+*	*1973-74+*	*Percentage change, 1971-72 to 1973-74 (top of range)*
Delaware				
University of Delaware	$1,100	$1,350	$1,560	42
Comprehensive universities and colleges (Delaware State College)	750	920	930	24
District of Columbia				
Comprehensive universities and colleges (Federal City College)	852	852	852	0
Florida				
Florida State University	1,620	1,620	1,620	0
University of Florida	1,620	1,620	1,620	0
Comprehensive universities and colleges	1,620	1,620	1,620	0
Georgia				
Georgia Institute of Technology	1,209	1,419	1,419	17
University of Georgia	1,025	1,239	1,259	23
Comprehensive universities and colleges	765-810	781-975	787-975	20
Hawaii				
University of Hawaii, Manoa	743	743	733	-1
Idaho				
University of Idaho	1,146	1,156	1,280	12
Comprehensive universities and colleges	§	840-1,296	840-1,296	§
Illinois				
Illinois State University	1,192	1,246	1,272	7
Northern Illinois University	1,229	1,235	§	§
Southern Illinois University, Carbondale	1,417	1,437	1,437	1
University of Illinois, Urbana-Champaign	1,416	1,676	1,676	18
Comprehensive universities and colleges	1,105-1,360	1,366-1,442	1,322-1,447	6
Liberal arts colleges (Sangamon State University)	1,110	1,110	1,133	2

TABLE 7 (cont.)

State and type of institution	*1971-72+*	*1972-73+*	*1973-74+*	*Percentage change, 1971-72 to 1973-74 (top of range)*
Indiana				
Ball State University	$1,080	$1,260	$1,260	17
Indiana University	1,490	1,490	1,560	5
Purdue University	1,600	1,600	1,600	0
Comprehensive universities and colleges (Indiana State University)	1,100	1,110	1,260	15
Iowa				
Iowa State University	1,230	1,230	1,332	8
University of Iowa	1,250	1,250	1,350	8
Comprehensive universities and colleges (University of Northern Iowa)	1,000	1,000	1,100	10
Kansas				
Kansas State University	1,066	1,066	1,316	23
University of Kansas	1,056	1,076	1,334	26
Comprehensive universities and colleges	777-1,039	781-1,060	885-1,327	28
Kentucky				
University of Kentucky	1,030	1,120	1,210	17
Comprehensive universities and colleges	800-876	875-896	950-955	9
Louisiana				
Louisiana State University, main campus	950	950	950	0
Comprehensive universities and colleges	630-948	525-956	530-964	2
Maine				
University of Maine, main campus	1,562	1,662	1,662	6
Comprehensive universities and colleges	1,300-1,316	1,400-1,466	1,400	6
Liberal arts colleges	§	1,300-1,430	1,300-1,430	§
Maryland				
University of Maryland, main campus	1,299	1,439	1,698	31
Comprehensive universities and colleges	450-715	655-954	970-1,179	65
Liberal arts colleges	692-1,389	710-1,300	720-1,560	12

TABLE 7 (cont.)

State and type of institution	*1971-72+*	*1972-73+*	*1973-74+*	*Percentage change, 1971-72 to 1973-74 (top of range)*
Massachusetts				
University of Massachusetts, main campus	$ 812	$1,069	$1,320	63
Comprehensive universities and colleges	600-678	600-700	600-820	21
Michigan				
Michigan State University	1,485	1,530	1,620	9
University of Michigan	2,140	2,260	2,600-2,800‡	31
Wayne State University	1,719	1,857	1,893	10
Western Michigan University	1,178	1,178	1,178	0
Comprehensive universities and colleges	1,023-1,457	1,110-1,502	1,240-1,562	7
Minnesota				
University of Minnesota, main campus	1,437	1,547	1,613	12
Comprehensive universities and colleges	§	555-834	508-873	§
Mississippi				
Mississippi State University	1,092	1,106	1,106	1
University of Mississippi	1,106	1,116	1,116	1
University of Southern Mississippi	1,077	1,077	1,077	0
Comprehensive universities and colleges	950-1,065	1,000-1,065	1,000-1,074	1
Missouri				
University of Missouri	1,420	1,540	1,540	8
Comprehensive universities and colleges	700-900	710-900	600-915	2
Liberal arts colleges (Missouri Western State College)	720	720	720	0
Montana				
Montana State University	1,318	1,318	1,376	4
University of Montana	1,318	1,318	1,387	5
Comprehensive universities and colleges	§	1,260-1,292	1,330-1,350	§
Nebraska				
University of Nebraska, main campus	1,260	1,210	1,210	-4
Comprehensive universities and colleges	631-731	651-731	§	§

TABLE 7 (cont.)

State and type of institution	*1971-72+*	*1972-73+*	*1973-74+*	*Percentage change, 1971-72 to 1973-74 (top of range)*
Nevada				
University of Nevada, main campus	$1,719	$1,719	$1,719	0
Comprehensive universities and colleges (University of Nevada, Las Vegas)	1,732	1,732	1,732	0
New Hampshire				
University of New Hampshire	2,084	2,233	2,233	7
Comprehensive universities and colleges	1,374-1,408	1,547-1,566	1,547-1,566	11
New Jersey				
Rutgers University, main campus	870	1,240	1,310	51
Comprehensive universities and colleges	700-850	1,171-1,339	1,171-1,339	58
New Mexico				
New Mexico State University	1,296	1,296	1,296	0
University of New Mexico	1,260	1,284	1,284	2
Comprehensive universities and colleges (Western New Mexico University)	450	900	900	100
New York				
State University of New York, university campuses	625	1,165-1,390‡	1,175-1,400‡	124
Comprehensive universities and colleges				
CUNY, Queens College	§	1,038	1,338	§
SUNY, college campuses	976-1,035	1,075-1,385‡	1,075-1,395‡	35
Liberal arts colleges	900-995	785-1,170‡	1,075-1,300‡	31
North Carolina				
North Carolina State University, main campus	1,502	2,002	2,034	35
University of North Carolina, main campus	1,477	1,772	1,997	35
Comprehensive universities and colleges	§	§	1,379-2,073	§

TABLE 7 (cont.)

State and type of institution	*1971-72+*	*1972-73+*	*1973-74+*	*Percentage change, 1971-72 to 1973-74 (top of range)*
North Dakota				
North Dakota State University	$1,044	$1,164	$1,164	11
University of North Dakota, main campus	1,064	1,184	1,184	11
Comprehensive universities and colleges	855-874	933-943	937-952	9
Liberal arts colleges (Mayville State College)	936	936	936	0
Ohio				
Kent State University	1,732	2,004	2,004	16
Miami University	1,800	1,980	1,980	10
Ohio State University	1,770	1,800	1,800	2
Comprehensive universities and colleges	§	1,050-1,650	1,188-1,680	§
Oklahoma				
Oklahoma State University	1,180	1,236	1,236	5
University of Oklahoma	1,200	1,200	1,200	0
Comprehensive universities and colleges	750-876	822-843	825-847	-3
Liberal arts colleges (Oklahoma College of Liberal Arts)	§	830	830	§
Oregon				
Oregon State University	1,542	1,565	1,718	11
University of Oregon	1,563	1,593	1,748	12
Comprehensive universities and colleges	1,203-1,206	1,233-1,239	1,392	15
Pennsylvania				
Pennsylvania State University	1,800	1,986	2,100	17
Temple University	1,870	1,870	1,950	4
University of Pittsburgh	1,972	1,972	2,002	2
Comprehensive universities and colleges (excluding Lincoln University)	1,290-1,470	1,380-1,470	1,380-1,576	7
Rhode Island				
University of Rhode Island	1,661	1,661	1,661	0
Comprehensive universities and colleges (Rhode Island College)	1,175	1,175	1,175	0

TABLE 7 (cont.)

State and type of institution	*1971-72+*	*1972-73+*	*1973-74+*	*Percentage change, 1971-72 to 1973-74 (top of range)*
South Carolina				
Clemson University	$1,340	$1,340	$1,340	0
University of South Carolina	1,260	1,280	1,280	2
Comprehensive universities and colleges (Winthrop College)	1,130	1,130	1,220	8
Liberal arts colleges (Francis Marion College)	910	910	910	0
South Dakota				
University of South Dakota	980	1,076	1,250	28
Comprehensive universities and colleges	792-975	765-1,132	930-1,337	37
Tennessee				
University of Tennessee, main campus	993	1,119	1,209	22
Comprehensive universities and colleges	888-998	1,038-1,116	1,128-1,226	23
Texas				
East Texas State University	1,330	1,330	1,402	5
North Texas State University	666	692	710	7
Texas A & M University	1,342	1,359	1,368	2
Texas Technical University	1,332	1,442	1,444	8
University of Houston	1,336	1,354	1,394	4
University of Texas, Austin	1,342	1,347	1,458	9
Comprehensive universities and colleges	470-1,378	1,200-1,360	1,200-1,380	0
Utah				
University of Utah	1,155	1,155	1,155	0
Utah State University	948	948	963	2
Comprehensive universities and colleges (Weber State College)	810	810	810	0
Vermont				
University of Vermont	2,528	2,536	2,688	6
Comprehensive universities and colleges (Castleton State College)	1,618	1,850	1,850	14
Liberal arts colleges	1,638	1,700	1,850	13

TABLE 7 (cont.)

State and type of institution	*1971-72*+	*1972-73*+	*1973-74*+	*Percentage change, 1971-72 to 1973-74 (top of range)*
Virginia				
University of Virginia, main campus	$1,217	$1,372	$1,447	19
Virginia Commonwealth University	1,034	1,080	1,190	15
Virginia Polytechnic Institute and State University	1,137	1,227	1,227	8
Comprehensive universities and colleges	810-1,310	813-1,360	870-1,410	8
Liberal arts colleges (Mary Washington College)	§	1,517	1,547	§
Washington				
University of Washington	1,359	1,581	1,581	16
Washington State University	1,359	1,581	1,581	16
Comprehensive universities and colleges	1,359	1,359	1,359	0
West Virginia				
West Virginia University	1,122	1,122	1,140	2
Comprehensive universities and colleges	506-1,077	515-1,082	990-1,082	0
Wisconsin				
University of Wisconsin, Madison and Milwaukee	1,900	1,906	1,906-2,006‡	6
Comprehensive universities and colleges	1,416-1,500	1,671-1,689	1,712-1,869‡	25
Wyoming				
University of Wyoming	1,357	1,377	1,377	1

*Institutions are classified in accordance with the Carnegie Commission Classification (Carnegie Commission, 1973*a*). All universities listed by name are classified as research universities or doctoral-granting universities in that classification. There are a few omissions because of absence of data. Under comprehensive universities and colleges and under liberal arts colleges, the name of the institution is included in parentheses if the data relate to only one institution (or campus).

+Where the charge reported for the preceding year differs from the charge originally reported for that year, we have used the more recently reported figure.

‡The lower figure applies to lower-division students; the higher figure applies to upper-division students. In the SUNY colleges and among comprehensive universities and colleges in Wisconsin, the charges vary somewhat from college to college, and the lower figure is usually the smallest charge applicable to lower-division students, while the higher figure is the largest charge applicable to upper-division students.

SOURCES: (1) National Association of State Universities and Land-Grant Colleges (annual); and (2) American Association of State Universities and Colleges (annual). We are indebted to staff members of these organizations for assistance in overcoming apparent inconsistencies in the data.

TABLE 8 Percentage of entering freshmen from each family income quintile, 1967 to 1973

Quintile	*1967*	*1968*	*1969*	*1970*	*1971*	*1972*	*1973*
Lowest	7.0%	9.4%	10.0%	10.2%	9.5%	13.1%	11.2%
Second	17.3	18.0	18.3	16.6	16.6	16.4	14.9
Third	19.9	21.5	21.5	20.7	22.0	22.7	23.7
Fourth	21.3	20.7	22.5	24.4	25.8	24.0	25.4
Highest	34.5	30.4	27.7	28.1	26.1	23.8	24.8
TOTAL	100.0	100.0	100.0	100.0	100.0	100.0	100.0

SOURCES: Freshman family income data from American Council on Education (annual); family income quintiles computed from data in U.S. Bureau of the Census (annual).

Quintiles for all families for 1967 and 1973 (estimated from 1972 data) are as follows (rounded to the nearest $50):

1967	*1973*
$0- 4,200	$0- 6,050
4,200- 6,850	6,050-10,000
6,850- 9,200	10,000-13,950
9,200-12,700	13,950-21,200
12,700 and over	21,200 and over

TABLE 9 Income distribution of young persons aged 18 to 24 and of undergraduates in the same age group enrolled in college, 1972-73

Family income group	*All persons aged 18 to 24*	*Undergraduates*
Less than $3,000	8.6%	4.1%
3,000 to 5,999	14.4	12.1
6,000 to 7,499	16.7	6.9
7,500 to 9,999	15.9	13.0
10,000 to 14,999	25.2	29.4
15,000 to 24,999	12.7	23.4
25,000 and over	6.5	11.1
TOTAL	100.0	100.0

SOURCE: National Commission on the Financing of Postsecondary Education (1973, p. 136).

TABLE 10 Per student family outlays for higher education, and per student subsidies

	Monetary outlays by family, per student				*Higher educational subsidies per student*			
Year	*Current dollars*		*Constant 1967 dollars*		*Current dollars*		*Constant 1967 dollars*	
1929-30	$ 563		$1,097		$ 310		$ 604	
1939-40	508		1,221		289		695	
1949-50	416	(751)	583	(1,052)	1,015	(680)	1,422	(953)
1959-60	966	(1,050)	1,107	(1,194)	951	(867)	1,088	(1,001)
1969-70	1,288	(1,401)	1,181	(1,294)	2,029	(1,916)	1,763	(1,650)

NOTE: Figures in parentheses are computed by excluding veterans' benefits paid to students from student aid. Since student aid adjustments reduce family outlays and increase subsidies, outlays are greater and subsidies smaller when veterans' benefits are omitted.

SOURCE: Carnegie Commission (1973*b*, p. 33).

TABLE 11 Average tuition and required fees and other student institutional expenses by type and control of institution, United States, 1973-74*

	Resi			
	Public			
Type of institution	*Tuition and fees*	*Room and board*	*Other expenses*	*Total budget*
Universities				
Research universities I	$627	$1,206	$679	$2,512
Research universities II	496	1,108	687	2,291
Other doctoral-granting universities I	558	1,130	682	2,370
Other doctoral-granting universities II	485	1,083	726	2,294
Comprehensive universities and colleges				
Comprehensive universities and colleges I	411	986	674	2,071
Comprehensive universities and colleges II	412	964	739	2,115

Private			
Tuition and fees	*Room and board*	*Other expenses*	*Total budget*
$3,050	$1,475	$514	$5,039
2,580	1,312	654	4,546
1,956	1,195	602	3,753
2,350	1,279	707	4,336
2,015	1,165	640	3,820
1,740	1,067	686	3,493

TABLE 11 (cont.)

Type of institution	Resident			
	Public			
	Tuition and fees	*Room and board*	*Other expenses*	*Total budget*
Liberal arts colleges				
Liberal arts colleges I	+	+	+	+
Liberal arts colleges II	420	1,165	899	2,484
Two-year institutions	302	1,005	627	1,934

*Averages are weighted by enrollment in each institution.

+There are only two public institutions in this category.

SOURCE: Allan and Suchar (1973); computations required to determine averages for each type of institution were carried out by the Carnegie Commission staff.

TABLE 12 Distribution of U.S. population by extent of participation in public higher education, income group, and time of participation, 1970 (in thousands)

	Family income, 1970				
	Less than $5,000	*$5,000-8,000*	*$8,000-11,500*	*$11,500-15,000*	*Over $15,000*
Full users					
Present	420	564	979	1,028	1,953
Past	1,332	1,787	3,103	3,260	6,190
Potential	2,648	3,551	6,167	6,479	12,303
Partial users					
Present	209	281	488	513	973
Past	890	1,193	2,072	2,177	4,134
Potential	1,134	1,521	2,643	2,776	5,272
Nonusers	30,040	26,161	28,163	22,531	18,275
TOTAL					

SOURCES: U.S. Bureau of the Census (1973, vol. 1, Tables 189, 197, 198, 199, 249, and 257). Data from Table 197 have been adjusted to account for the enrollment of students whose age exceeds 34 years.

Private			
Tuition and fees	*Room and board*	*Other expenses*	*Total budget*
2,510	1,182	519	4,211
1,728	1,027	515	3,270
1,382	1,085	430	2,897

Persons	
Number	*Percent*
4,944	2.4
15,672	7.7
31,148	15.3
2,464	1.2
10,466	5.2
13,346	6.6
125,170	61.6
203,210	100.0

A Technical Note on Tables 2, 4, and 5

There is no method of estimating the proportion of educational expenses covered by tuition entirely accurately from available data. The measure we have used–revenue from tuition and required fees as a percentage of educational expenditures less organized research–is probably the most satisfactory available, but there are problems associated with its use, relating especially to universities, that have been discussed in the text (pp. 20 to 23). An additional problem is that funds drawn from educational accounts are sometimes used for student aid and are included among educational expenditures.

Furthermore, the data for 1971-72, which we used because they were the most recent financial statistics available, were obtained from tapes in the data bank developed by the National Commission on the Financing of Postsecondary Education. The institutional financial data provided to the National Commission by the U.S. National Center for Educational Statistics had not been edited at the time they were turned over to the Commission. We were able to obtain data from the University of Massachusetts and from the State University of New York to correct errors or omissions relating to those two institutions, but there may be other errors in the data which we did not detect because they were less obvious.

An alternative measure used in the report to which this is a supplement (Carnegie Commission, 1973*b*) is revenue from tuition and required fees as a percentage of revenue received for educational purposes. Because institutions normally spend all the income they receive in any given year, revenue received for educational purposes does not ordinarily differ appreciably from educational expenditures. However, in recent years, a good many institutions of higher education have incurred deficits (usually involving drawing from endowment funds), and thus revenue received for educational purposes may be significantly smaller than educational expenditures.

There is another measure that might have been used, but it, too, involves difficulties. This is the actual charge for tuition and required fees per full-time-equivalent student as a percentage of educational costs per full-time-equivalent student. In order to arrive at a measure that relates to undergraduate education, the number of postbaccalaureate students can be weighted, in computing educational costs per FTE student, to reflect the relatively high costs of postbaccalaureate education. However, there is some disagreement among experts as to the appropriate weights to be used for this purpose, especially in view of the fact that the costs of undergraduate and of graduate education are frequently joint costs that cannot be clearly separated.

In developing the adjusted estimate of 26 to 27 percent discussed on page 23, designed to measure more closely the actual percentage applicable to undergraduates in public four-year institutions, we made use of both the first and third measures discussed above and then averaged the differing results obtained. Our original measure of revenue from tuition and required fees as a percentage of educational expenditure was adjusted to eliminate the exceptionally high educational expenditures in medical schools and a portion of the high expenditures for graduate education. Alternatively, we computed actual resident tuition and fees per full-time student as a percentage of educational costs per full-time student, using appropriately high weights for medical education and advanced graduate education, as well as a weight of two to one for graduate education at the master's level. The results of these procedures, of course, altered the percentage obtained for public universities substantially more than for comprehensive universities and colleges. The adjusted figure for public universities may be as high as about 30 percent.

Attachment A

Comments of Commissioner Ernest L. Boyer
Joining in Agreement Are:
Commissioner Marian W. LaFollette;
Commissioner Louis P. Rodriquez;
Commissioner John W. Porter; and
Commissioner Ruth C. Silva

The Financing of Postsecondary Education

A Framework for Future Planning

The National Commission on the Financing of Postsecondary Education has completed its work, and the report has been unanimously endorsed. The Commission has responded imaginatively and well to its legislative mandate. Especially commendable has been the development of an analytical framework which makes it possible for policymakers to assess, at least in part, the impact of a financing proposal *before* it is introduced.

While applauding the report, I am convinced we have yet another obligation to fulfill. During our study it became quite clear to the Commission that the postsecondary education financing debate has generated misunderstandings at all levels. There are strong advocates on all sides, and each new proposal seems to generate more heat than light.

Given this confusion, I believe we should speak to some of the hotly contested issues, not by introducing our own detailed financing plan, but rather by setting forth a series of propositions on which policymakers might agree or disagree.

We have worked 12 months on this timely topic. We gathered information, heard testimony from many witnesses, and discussed together the findings of our study. It seems appropriate, if not essential, that we share some of the convictions that have emerged and make clear that in our own opinion the various financing strategies discussed in the report are not of equal merit.

Therefore, I wish to append to our formal report a series of statements—call them guiding principles, if you will—which may help to sharpen the policy issues to be faced. Many of the propositions simply summarize current practices, while others are not as broadly endorsed. It is my opinion, however, that these statements will be helpful as a partial structure within which various financing proposals can be tested and will serve in part as a framework for future planning.

I. STATE AND LOCAL SUPPORT OF POSTSECONDARY EDUCATION

A. State and local governments have the primary public responsibility of providing basic institutional aid to postsecondary education.

B. Public institutions, as a general rule, should receive their primary institutional support from state and local governments.

Such support should be adequate to maintain an excellent and diversified network of two-year, baccalaureate and graduate institutions in each state.

State and local support should be sufficient to make it possible for public institutions to provide two-years of postsecondary education to all qualified students, preferably at no cost to the student, but at least at tuition rates not exceeding present levels.

Each state should provide public institutions with the financial assistance needed to support a diversified upper baccalaureate and graduate educational program, although students might contribute moderately to the support of this more advanced, higher cost instruction.

State and local governments should share with the federal government in the funding of basic research and public service programs at public institutions.

C. Private institutions, while receiving their principal support from non-public sources, should be recognized as essential educational resources by each state.

Direct institutional grants to private institutions should be seriously considered by the several states. The method of providing such direct aid to private institutions, while varying from state to state, should, nonetheless, be linked to the performance of specifically identified public missions.

Four such arrangements are suggested:

High priority educational programs: Private institutions might receive public aid in support of high priority instructional programs, such as the expansion of medical and dental education, contractual support for specialized degree offerings not available in the public sector, or for the joint purchase and use of resources of high cost services such as library acquisitions and computer facilities.

Cost-of-Instruction Allowances: Private institutions might receive cost-of-instruction allowances for educating certain special categories of students, such as veterans, the handicapped and the financially disadvantaged.

Expansion of Enrollment: Private institutions might receive public support for increasing their enrollment at the lower or upper levels and thus better utilizing available facilities within the private sector.

Lower Division Students: Private institutions might receive a grant for each state resident they enroll at the freshman and sophomore levels, thus joining with the public sector in the fulfillment of the commitment to two years of postsecondary education.

D. Both public and private institutions should accept procedures which provide reasonable accountability while at the same time preserving essential institutional integrity. Private institutions receiving public funds should accept financial and programmatic reporting systems, which while not as extensive as those required of public institutions, nonetheless allow professional judgments to be made concerning their financial conditions and the quality of their services.

E. Ranges of acceptable funding levels for private institutions receiving public support might cooperatively be developed to meet the imperatives of public accountability while protecting institutional flexibility and identity.

II. FEDERAL SUPPORT OF POSTSECONDARY EDUCATION

A. The federal government has a critically significant supportive role to play in the financing of both public and private postsecondary education.

B. Federal aid to postsecondary education should complement the financing obligations of state and local governments. Specifically, such funding should support programs which are truly national in character and transcend the interests or needs of any given state or region.

Four major federal obligations to postsecondary education are proposed.

Equality of Access: *The federal government should promote equality of access to postsecondary education through grants to students and institutions which will enable both full and part-time students from low and middle income families to enroll in and complete an appropriate postsecondary education program.*

The federal government also should subsidize work-study and loan programs for those students, especially at the upper and graduate levels, who must finance their own education.

Research and Graduate Education: *The federal government should selectively support, through direct institutional grants and aid to graduate students, high quality research and graduate education in order to develop the nation's intellectual resources and to identify and resolve problems which transcend the several states.*

High Priority Professional Fields: *The federal government should support through institutional and student grants, a limited number of high priority professional fields of study (for example, medicine) which are directly linked to national needs.*

Educational Reform: *The federal government should provide grants to institutions to stimulate reforms in education which will make it possible for institutions to alter their instructional and managerial practices in response to major social and educational change.*

III. STUDENT AND FAMILY SUPPORT OF POSTSECONDARY EDUCATION

A. Students and their families should share somewhat in the cost of postsecondary education, in both the public and private sectors, although the level of such support will differ in each.

B. In the public sector, income through tuition and other fees should remain a secondary source of institutional support.

Tuition for the first two years of public education beyond high school should be free or at least be stabilized at the present level.

Beyond the first two years, a tuition schedule, graduated by level, might be introduced. Such a schedule, however, should remain low in cost (a maximum of approximately one-third of instructional costs might be a useful bench mark) and should increase only at the annual rate of inflation.

C. In the private sector, income through tuition should remain the primary source of institutional support.

A program of federally financed student assistance, augmented by the states, should be provided to low and middle income students to offset somewhat the higher tuition charges of private institutions.

D. In both public and private sector institutions, students and their families should be expected to pay according to their financial ability for most of the cost of ancillary services (parking, health care) which are only indirectly related or unrelated to their basic instructional program.

IV. PHILANTHROPIC SUPPORT OF POSTSECONDARY EDUCATION

A. The philanthropic contributions of alumni, foundations, organizations and individuals to both public and private institutions should be expanded.

B. The federal and state governments should maintain appropriate tax incentives to assure the continuation and expansion of philanthropic contributions to postsecondary education.

C. Contributors to postsecondary education should be encouraged to include unrestricted gifts in their donations in order to permit maximum flexibility in the use of such income and to preserve institutional integrity.

V. CONCLUSION

In summary, I believe the time has come to develop a cohesive and rationally developed set of principles for financing postsecondary education. This comprehensive financing strategy should maintain a constructive balance both within and between the public and private sectors, while enhancing the diversity of our institutional missions.

The preceding propositions are intended to be illustrative, not exhaustive, and are set forth here to help sharpen our thinking and to enhance rather than detract from the Commission's report.

Attachment B

OFFICE OF THE CHANCELLOR
Claremont University Center
Claremont, California 91711

August 20, 1973

Mr. Allan W. Ostar
AMERICAN ASSOCIATION OF STATE
COLLEGES AND UNIVERSITIES
One Dupont Circle, Suite 700
Washington, D.C. 20036

Dear Allan:

I appreciated receiving a copy of your letter to the TIMES about the Carnegie report on *Higher Education: Who Pays? Who Benefits? Who Should Pay?* I strongly sympathize with your position in favor of low tuitions.

At the same time, I am in general agreement with the main thrust of the Carnegie report. Indeed, about a year ago I reached essentially the same position in my ERIC paper *Who Benefits from Higher Education and Who Should Pay?*

As I have considered the financing of higher education over the past five years, I have come to three basic conclusions. The first is that many conflicting values are at stake, and that inevitably a good solution must be a compromise among them resulting in a system of finance not unlike that which we now have. In this system, about two-thirds of the economic cost (including forgone income) is borne by students and their families and one-third by taxpayers and philanthropists. This division is precisely what the Carnegie report recommends. The second conclusion is that there must be some points of low-cost or no-cost access to the system. This the report provides for by recommending very low tuitions in the Community Colleges. I would prefer to add the state colleges to the very low tuition category for the reason that the state colleges operate at low cost per student and cater to low-income families. (See the Carnegie report, p. 90.) The third conclusion is that the tuition gap between the public and private institutions should be narrowed primarily by strengthening the position of the privates, not by imposing high tuitions on the publics. The report accepts this concept.

So, in broad outline, I find the document, congenial to my thinking. It can be argued that it is a first step on the road to high or full-cost tuitions, and that may be. For those wishing to hold tuitions down, as I do, the best polemical strategy may be to argue for reducing tuitions and not admitting that they might properly be raised even a little. But I think this would be polemical strategy and not a facing of the reality of conflicting values among which compromise must be found.

I am also coming to the view that higher eduation is simply not going to get enough support from taxes and gifts to keep afloat, and that there is no alternative to some increase in tuitions. I can live with the Carnegie program, whereas I cannot accept many other proposals—especially those of economists who are in love with the price system but have not thought through all aspects of the problems and needs of higher education.

The trouble with the two-thirds/one-thirds formulation is that the result depends largely on the estimate of foregone income. I think the Carnegie Commission has underestimated. The result is that their residual to be met by tuition is greater than mine. Nevertheless, I am not too offended by their basic result because their moderation is in sharp contrast to the extreme views that have been expressed by many economists and by many federal and state officials.

I also question their recommendation that tuitions should be varied by levels of education (low tuition for freshmen and sophomores, medium for juniors and seniors, and high for graduate and professional students). It presents some serious practical problems. It would tend to drive upper division students out of private institutions, it would increase the dropout rate for minority and other low-income students in all types of institutions, and it would compound problems of graduate study and of certain professional fields; e.g., theology. Varying tuitions by level of instruction might also be an opening wedge for the NCHEMS approach to cost and price policy. For a variety of educational reasons, (relating to student choices, problems of cost allocation, and the very concept of a unified university) I am concerned about efforts to price specific educational services on the basis of computed unit costs.

I am taking the liberty of enclosing a paper I have prepared for the CED in which I outline in some detail the reasons for my "moderate" line. This paper is in process of publication.

Forgive me for responding at such great length. Warm personal regards,

Yours sincerely,

Howard R. Bowen
Chancellor

References

Allan, J. B., and E. W. Suchar: *Student Expenses at Postsecondary Institutions,* College Entrance Examination Board, New York, 1973.

American Association of State Universities and Colleges: *Student Charges,* Washington, D.C., annual (title varies).

American Council on Education: *Higher Education and National Affairs,* vol. 23, no. 7, Feb. 15, 1974.

American Council on Education: *National Norms for Entering College Freshmen,* Washington, D.C., annual (title varies).

Bowen, H. R.: "Financing Higher Education: The Current State of the Debate," paper presented before the National Council of Independent Colleges and Universities, St. Louis, Mo., Jan. 15, 1974.

Carnegie Commission on Higher Education: *Quality and Equality: Revised Recommendations, New Levels of Federal Responsibility for Higher Education,* McGraw-Hill Book Company, New York, 1970.

Carnegie Commission on Higher Education: *The Capitol and the Campus: State Responsibility for Postsecondary Education,* McGraw-Hill Book Company, New York, 1971.

Carnegie Commission on Higher Education: *Institutional Aid: Federal Support to Colleges and Universities,* McGraw-Hill Book Company, New York, 1972.

Carnegie Commission on Higher Education: *A Classification of Institutions of Higher Education,* Berkeley, Calif., 1973*a*.

Carnegie Commission on Higher Education: *Higher Education: Who Pays? Who Benefits? Who Should Pay?,* McGraw-Hill Book Company, New York, 1973*b*.

College Entrance Examination Board: *Report of the Committee on Student Economics,* New York, 1972.

Committee for Economic Development: *The Management and Financing of Colleges,* New York, 1973.

National Association of State Universities and Land-Grant Colleges: *Tuition, Required Fees, Room and Board Charges,* Washington, D.C., annual (title varies).

National Commission on the Financing of Postsecondary Education: *Financing Postsecondary Education in the United States,* Washington, D.C., 1973.

O'Neill, J. A.: *Sources of Funds to Colleges and Universities,* Carnegie Commission on Higher Education, Berkeley, California, 1973.

Pennsylvania Association of Colleges and Universities: *A Proposal for Financing Higher Education in the Commonwealth,* November 1973.

Task Force on Financing Higher Education: *Higher Education in New York State: A Report to Governor Nelson A. Rockefeller,* Albany, 1973.

U.S. Bureau of the Census: "Money Income of Families and Persons in the United States," *Current Population Survey,* series P-60, nos. 59, 66, 75, 80, 85, and 90, Washington, D.C., annual (title varies).

U.S. Bureau of the Census: *1970 Census of Population, United States Summary, Detailed Characteristics,* Washington, D.C., 1973.

U.S. National Center for Educational Statistics: *Fall Enrollment in Higher Education 1970: Supplementary Information: Institutional Data,* Washington, D.C., 1971.

U.S. National Center for Educational Statistics: *Projections of Educational Statistics to 1980-81,* 1971 ed., Washington, D.C., 1972.

U.S. National Center for Educational Statistics: *Digest of Educational Statistics, 1972,* Washington, D.C., 1973.

U.S. President: *Economic Report of the President: Transmitted to the Congress, January 1972,* Washington, D.C., 1972.

U.S. President: *Economic Report of the President: Transmitted to the Congress, January 1974,* Washington, D.C., 1974.

Van Dyne, L.: "Michigan Students Protest Tuition Increases. . .," *Chronicle of Higher Education,* Nov. 12, 1973, p. 5.

Carnegie Commission on Higher Education

Sponsored Research Studies

The following publications are available from McGraw-Hill Book Company, Box 402, Hightstown, New Jersey, 08520.

THE ACADEMIC SYSTEM
IN AMERICAN SOCIETY
Alain Touraine

HIGHER EDUCATION
AND THE LABOR MARKET
Margaret S. Gordon (ed.)

THE ACADEMIC MELTING POT
Stephen Steinberg

LEADERSHIP AND AMBIGUITY:
THE AMERICAN COLLEGE PRESIDENT
Michael D. Cohen and James G. March

CONTENT AND CONTEXT:
ESSAYS ON COLLEGE EDUCATION
Carl Kaysen (ed.)

EDUCATION FOR THE PROFESSIONS
OF MEDICINE, LAW, THEOLOGY, AND
SOCIAL WELFARE
Everett C. Hughes, Barrie Thorne, Agostino M. DeBaggis, Arnold Gurin, and David Williams

THE FUTURE OF HIGHER EDUCATION:
SOME SPECULATIONS AND SUGGESTIONS
Alexander M. Mood

THE RISE OF THE ARTS
ON THE AMERICAN CAMPUS
Jack Morrison

THE UNIVERSITY AND THE CITY:
EIGHT CASES OF INVOLVEMENT
George Nash, Dan Waldorf, and Robert E. Price

THE BEGINNING OF THE FUTURE: A
HISTORICAL APPROACH TO GRADUATE
EDUCATION IN THE ARTS AND SCIENCES
Richard J. Storr

ACADEMIC TRANSFORMATION:
SEVENTEEN INSTITUTIONS UNDER
PRESSURE
David Riesman and Verne A. Stadtman (eds.)

THE UNIVERSITY AS AN ORGANIZATION
James A. Perkins (ed.)

WHERE COLLEGES ARE AND
WHO ATTENDS:
EFFECTS OF ACCESSIBILITY ON
COLLEGE ATTENDANCE
C. Arnold Anderson, Mary Jean Bowman and Vincent Tinto

THE EMERGING TECHNOLOGY:
INSTRUCTIONAL USE OF THE
COMPUTER IN HIGHER
EDUCATION
Roger E. Levien

NEW DIRECTIONS IN LEGAL
EDUCATION
Herbert L. Packer and Thomas Ehrlich

A STATISTICAL PORTRAIT OF
HIGHER EDUCATION
Seymour E. Harris

EDUCATION AND EVANGELISM:
A PROFILE OF PROTESTANT COLLEGES
C. Robert Pace

THE HOME OF SCIENCE:
THE ROLE OF THE UNIVERSITY
Dael Wolfle

PROFESSIONAL EDUCATION:
SOME NEW DIRECTIONS
Edgar H. Schein

THE NONPROFIT RESEARCH
INSTITUTE: ITS ORIGIN, OPERATION,
PROBLEMS, AND PROSPECTS
Harold Orlans

THE INVISIBLE COLLEGES:
A PROFILE OF SMALL, PRIVATE
COLLEGES WITH LIMITED RESOURCES
Alexander W. Astin and Calvin B. T. Lee

AMERICAN HIGHER EDUCATION:
DIRECTIONS OLD AND NEW
Joseph Ben-David

A DEGREE AND WHAT ELSE?:
CORRELATES AND CONSEQUENCES OF A COLLEGE EDUCATION
Stephen B. Withey, Jo Anne Coble, Gerald Gurin, John P. Robinson, Burkhard Strumpel, Elizabeth Keogh Taylor, and Arthur C. Wolfe

THE MULTICAMPUS UNIVERSITY:
A STUDY OF ACADEMIC GOVERNANCE
Eugene C. Lee and Frank M. Bowen

INSTITUTIONS IN TRANSITION:
A PROFILE OF CHANGE IN HIGHER EDUCATION
(INCORPORATING THE 1970 STATISTICAL REPORT)
Harold L. Hodgkinson

EFFICIENCY IN LIBERAL EDUCATION:
A STUDY OF COMPARATIVE INSTRUCTIONAL COSTS FOR DIFFERENT WAYS OF ORGANIZING TEACHING-LEARNING IN A LIBERAL ARTS COLLEGE
Howard R. Bowen and Gordon K. Douglass

CREDIT FOR COLLEGE:
PUBLIC POLICY FOR STUDENT LOANS
Robert W. Hartman

MODELS AND MAVERICKS:
A PROFILE OF PRIVATE LIBERAL ARTS COLLEGES
Morris T. Keeton

BETWEEN TWO WORLDS:
A PROFILE OF NEGRO HIGHER EDUCATION
Frank Bowles and Frank A. DeCosta

BREAKING THE ACCESS BARRIERS:
A PROFILE OF TWO-YEAR COLLEGES
Leland L. Medsker and Dale Tillery

ANY PERSON, ANY STUDY:
AN ESSAY ON HIGHER EDUCATION IN THE UNITED STATES
Eric Ashby

THE NEW DEPRESSION IN HIGHER EDUCATION:
A STUDY OF FINANCIAL CONDITIONS AT 41 COLLEGES AND UNIVERSITIES
Earl F. Cheit

FINANCING MEDICAL EDUCATION:
AN ANALYSIS OF ALTERNATIVE POLICIES AND MECHANISMS
Rashi Fein and Gerald I. Weber

HIGHER EDUCATION IN NINE COUNTRIES:
A COMPARATIVE STUDY OF COLLEGES AND UNIVERSITIES ABROAD
Barbara B. Burn, Philip G. Altbach, Clark Kerr, and James A. Perkins

BRIDGES TO UNDERSTANDING:
INTERNATIONAL PROGRAMS OF AMERICAN COLLEGES AND UNIVERSITIES
Irwin T. Sanders and Jennifer C. Ward

GRADUATE AND PROFESSIONAL EDUCATION, 1980:
A SURVEY OF INSTITUTIONAL PLANS
Lewis B. Mayhew

THE AMERICAN COLLEGE AND AMERICAN CULTURE:
SOCIALIZATION AS A FUNCTION OF HIGHER EDUCATION
Oscar Handlin and Mary F. Handlin

RECENT ALUMNI AND HIGHER EDUCATION:
A SURVEY OF COLLEGE GRADUATES
Joe L. Spaeth and Andrew M. Greeley

CHANGE IN EDUCATIONAL POLICY:
SELF-STUDIES IN SELECTED COLLEGES AND UNIVERSITIES
Dwight R. Ladd

STATE OFFICIALS AND HIGHER EDUCATION:
A SURVEY OF THE OPINIONS AND EXPECTATIONS OF POLICY MAKERS IN NINE STATES
Heinz Eulau and Harold Quinley

ACADEMIC DEGREE STRUCTURES:
INNOVATIVE APPROACHES
PRINCIPLES OF REFORM IN DEGREE STRUCTURES IN THE UNITED STATES
Stephen H. Spurr

COLLEGES OF THE FORGOTTEN AMERICANS:
A PROFILE OF STATE COLLEGES AND REGIONAL UNIVERSITIES
E. Alden Dunham

FROM BACKWATER TO MAINSTREAM:
A PROFILE OF CATHOLIC HIGHER EDUCATION
Andrew M. Greeley

THE ECONOMICS OF THE MAJOR PRIVATE UNIVERSITIES
William G. Bowen
(Out of print, but available from University Microfilms.)

THE FINANCE OF HIGHER EDUCATION
Howard R. Bowen
(Out of print, but available from University Microfilms.)

ALTERNATIVE METHODS OF FEDERAL FUNDING FOR HIGHER EDUCATION
Ron Wolk
(Out of print, but available from University Microfilms.)

INVENTORY OF CURRENT RESEARCH ON HIGHER EDUCATION 1968
Dale M. Heckman and Warren Bryan Martin
(Out of print, but available from University Microfilms.)

The following technical reports are available from the Carnegie Commission on Higher Education, 2150 Shattuck Avenue, Berkeley, California 94704.

THE DEMISE OF DIVERSITY?
A COMPARATIVE PROFILE OF EIGHT TYPES OF INSTITUTIONS
C. Robert Pace

FLYING A LEARNING CENTER:
DESIGN AND COSTS OF AN OFF-CAMPUS SPACE FOR LEARNING
Thomas J. Karwin

POLITICAL IDEOLOGIES OF GRADUATE STUDENTS:
CRYSTALLIZATION, CONSISTENCY, AND CONTEXTUAL EFFECTS
Margaret A. Fay and Jeff A. Weintraub

A CLASSIFICATION OF INSTITUTIONS OF HIGHER EDUCATION

PROFESSORS, UNIONS, AND AMERICAN HIGHER EDUCATION
Everett Carll Ladd, Jr. and Seymour Martin Lipset

SOURCES OF FUNDS TO COLLEGES AND UNIVERSITIES
June O'Neill

THE NEW DEPRESSION IN HIGHER EDUCATION—TWO YEARS LATER
Earl F. Cheit

ESTIMATING THE RETURNS TO EDUCATION:
A DISAGGREGATED APPROACH
Richard S. Eckaus
(Out of print, but available from University Microfilms.)

AN INVENTORY OF ACADEMIC INNOVATION AND REFORM
Ann Heiss
(Out of print, but available from University Microfilms.)

TRENDS AND PROJECTIONS OF PHYSICIANS IN THE UNITED STATES 1967-2002
Mark S. Blumberg

PAPERS ON EFFICIENCY IN THE MANAGEMENT OF HIGHER EDUCATION
Alexander M. Mood, Colin Bell, Lawrence Bogard, Helen Brownlee, and Joseph McCloskey
(Out of print, but available from University Microfilms.)

AMERICAN COLLEGE AND UNIVERSITY ENROLLMENT TRENDS IN 1971
Richard E. Peterson
(Out of print, but available from University Microfilms.)

MAY 1970: THE CAMPUS AFTERMATH OF CAMBODIA AND KENT STATE
Richard E. Peterson and John A. Bilorusky

RESOURCE USE IN HIGHER EDUCATION: TRENDS IN OUTPUT AND INPUTS, 1930-1967
June O'Neill
(Out of print, but available from University Microfilms.)

MENTAL ABILITY AND HIGHER EDUCATIONAL ATTAINMENT IN THE 20TH CENTURY
Paul Taubman and Terence Wales
(Out of print, but available from University Microfilms.)

The following reprints are available from the Carnegie Commission on Higher Education, 2150 Shattuck Avenue, Berkeley, California 94704. (First copies of reprints are sent free on request. Enclose 20 cents each for additional copies to defray costs of postage and handling.)

PROBLEMS IN THE TRANSITION FROM ELITE TO MASS HIGHER EDUCATION, *by Martin Trow. A paper prepared for a conference on mass higher education sponsored by the Organisation for Economic Co-operation and Development, June 1973.*

MEASURING FACULTY UNIONISM: QUANTITY AND QUALITY, *by Bill Aussieker and J. W. Garbarino, reprinted from* INDUSTRIAL RELATIONS, *vol. 12, no. 2, May 1973.*

COMING OF MIDDLE AGE IN HIGHER EDUCATION, *by Earl F. Cheit, address delivered to American Association of State Colleges and Universities and National Association of State Universities and Land-Grant Colleges, Washington, D.C., November 13, 1972.*

THE DISTRIBUTION OF ACADEMIC TENURE IN AMERICAN HIGHER EDUCATION, *by Martin Trow, reprinted from Bardwell Smith (ed.),* THE TENURE DEBATE, *Jossey-Bass, San Francisco, 1972.*

THE NATURE AND ORIGINS OF THE CARNEGIE COMMISSION ON HIGHER EDUCATION, *by Alan Pifer, based on a speech delivered to the Pennsylvania Association of Colleges and Universities, Oct. 16, 1972, reprinted by permission of The Carnegie Foundation for the Advancement of Teaching.*

MORE FOR LESS: HIGHER EDUCATION'S NEW PRIORITY, *by Virginia B. Smith, reprinted from* UNIVERSAL HIGHER EDUCATION: COSTS AND BENEFITS, *American Council on Education, Washington, D.C., 1971.*

ACADEMIA AND POLITICS IN AMERICA, *by Seymour M. Lipset, reprinted from Thomas J. Nossiter (ed.),* IMAGINATION AND PRECISION IN THE SOCIAL SCIENCES, *pp. 211-289, Faber and Faber, London, 1972.*

POLITICS OF ACADEMIC NATURAL SCIENTISTS AND ENGINEERS, *by Everett C. Ladd, Jr., and Seymour M. Lipset, reprinted from Science,* vol. 176, no. 4039, pp. 1091-1100, June 9, 1972.

THE INTELLECTUAL AS CRITIC AND REBEL: WITH SPECIAL REFERENCE TO THE UNITED STATES AND THE SOVIET UNION, *by Seymour M. Lipset and Richard B. Dobson, reprinted from* DAEDALUS, *vol. 101, no. 3, pp. 137-198, Summer 1972.*

POLITICS OF AMERICAN SOCIOLOGISTS, *by Seymour M. Lipset and Everett C. Ladd, Jr., reprinted from* AMERICAN JOURNAL OF SOCIOLOGY, *vol. 78, no. 1, pp. 67-104, July 1972.*

FACULTY UNIONISM: FROM THEORY TO PRACTICE, *by Joseph W. Garbarino, reprinted from* INDUSTRIAL RELATIONS, *vol. 11, no. 1, pp. 1-17, February 1972.*

INTERNATIONAL PROGRAMS OF U.S. COLLEGES AND UNIVERSITIES: PRIORITIES FOR THE SEVENTIES, *by James A. Perkins, Occasional Paper No. 1, July 1971, reprinted by permission of the International Council for Educational Development.*

ACCELERATED PROGRAMS OF MEDICAL EDUCATION, *by Mark S. Blumberg, reprinted from* JOURNAL OF MEDICAL EDUCATION, *vol. 46, no. 8, August 1971.**

SCIENTIFIC MANPOWER FOR 1970-1985, *by Allan M. Cartter, reprinted from* SCIENCE, *vol. 172, no. 3979, pp. 132-140, April 9, 1971.*

A NEW METHOD OF MEASURING STATES' HIGHER EDUCATION BURDEN, *by Neil Timm, reprinted from* THE JOURNAL OF HIGHER EDUCATION, *vol. 42, no. 1, pp. 27-33, January 1971.**

REGENT WATCHING, *by Earl F. Cheit, reprinted from* AGB REPORTS, *vol. 13, no. 6, pp. 4-13, March 1971.**

COLLEGE GENERATIONS–FROM THE 1930's TO THE 1960's, *by Seymour M. Lipset and Everett C. Ladd, Jr., reprinted from* THE PUBLIC INTEREST, *no. 24, Summer 1971.*

AMERICAN SOCIAL SCIENTISTS AND THE GROWTH OF CAMPUS POLITICAL ACTIVISM IN THE 1960s, *by Everett C. Ladd, Jr., and Seymour M. Lipset, reprinted from* SOCIAL SCIENCES INFORMATION, *vol. 10, no. 2, April 1971.*

THE POLITICS OF AMERICAN POLITICAL SCIENTISTS, *by Everett C. Ladd, Jr., and Seymour M. Lipset, reprinted from PS, vol. 4, no. 2, Spring 1971.**

THE DIVIDED PROFESSORIATE, *by Seymour M. Lipset and Everett C. Ladd, Jr., reprinted from* CHANGE, *vol. 3, no. 3, pp. 54-60, May 1971.**

JEWISH ACADEMICS IN THE UNITED STATES: THEIR ACHIEVEMENTS, CULTURE AND POLITICS, *by Seymour M. Lipset and Everett C. Ladd, Jr., reprinted from* AMERICAN JEWISH YEAR BOOK, *1971.*

THE UNHOLY ALLIANCE AGAINST THE CAMPUS, *by Kenneth Keniston and Michael Lerner, reprinted from* NEW YORK TIMES MAGAZINE, *November 8, 1970.*

PRECARIOUS PROFESSORS: NEW PATTERNS OF REPRESENTATION, *by Joseph W. Garbarino, reprinted from* INDUSTRIAL RELATIONS, *vol. 10, no. 1, February 1971.**

. . . AND WHAT PROFESSORS THINK: ABOUT STUDENT PROTEST AND MANNERS, MORALS, POLITICS, AND CHAOS ON THE CAMPUS, *by Seymour Martin Lipset and Everett Carll Ladd, Jr., reprinted from* PSYCHOLOGY TODAY, *November 1970.**

DEMAND AND SUPPLY IN U.S. HIGHER EDUCATION: A PROGRESS REPORT, *by Roy Radner and Leonard S. Miller, reprinted from* AMERICAN ECONOMIC REVIEW, *May 1970.**

RESOURCES FOR HIGHER EDUCATION: AN ECONOMIST'S VIEW, *by Theodore W. Schultz, reprinted from* JOURNAL OF POLITICAL ECONOMY, *vol. 76, no. 3, University of Chicago, May/June 1968.**

INDUSTRIAL RELATIONS AND UNIVERSITY RELATIONS, *by Clark Kerr, reprinted from* PROCEEDINGS OF THE 21ST ANNUAL WINTER MEETING OF THE INDUSTRIAL RELATIONS RESEARCH ASSOCIATION, *pp. 15-25.**

NEW CHALLENGES TO THE COLLEGE AND UNIVERSITY, *by Clark Kerr, reprinted from Kermit Gordon (ed.),* AGENDA FOR THE NATION, *The Brookings Institution, Washington, D.C., 1968.**

PRESIDENTIAL DISCONTENT, *by Clark Kerr, reprinted from David C. Nichols (ed.),* PERSPECTIVES ON CAMPUS TENSIONS: PAPERS PREPARED FOR THE SPECIAL COMMITTEE ON CAMPUS TENSIONS, *American Council on Education, Washington, D.C., September 1970.**

STUDENT PROTEST–AN INSTITUTIONAL AND NATIONAL PROFILE, *by Harold Hodgkinson, reprinted from* THE RECORD, *vol. 71, no. 4, May 1970.**

WHAT'S BUGGING THE STUDENTS?, *by Kenneth Keniston, reprinted from* EDUCATIONAL RECORD, *American Council on Education, Washington, D.C., Spring 1970.**

THE POLITICS OF ACADEMIA, *by Seymour Martin Lipset, reprinted from David C. Nichols (ed.),* PERSPECTIVES ON CAMPUS TENSIONS: PAPERS PREPARED FOR THE SPECIAL COMMITTEE ON CAMPUS TENSIONS, *American Council on Education, Washington, D.C., September 1970.**

**The Commission's stock of this reprint has been exhausted.*